Praise for

Even the Odds

and Karen Firestone

"Risk is everywhere, and we all need to manage it wisely. This book teaches you to manage risk as a highly proficient and articulate investment professional does. Karen Firestone shares her copious experience in a series of useful and engaging examples."

—Ben Shapiro, Malcolm P. McNair Professor of Marketing,
Emeritus, at the Harvard Business School

"There is no other book like *Even the Odds*. It is a must-read for every MBA student launching a career and every midcareer professional contemplating what is next. This book spans risk/reward tradeoffs with uncommon candor, clarity, and cleverness. It blends Warren Buffet's wisdom with the engaging personal appeal of Oprah Winfrey. Written by one of the world's most successful and witty money managers, this book adroitly navigates the opportunities in the turmoil of markets and money as well as in the complexities of love, family, and community life. Unlike the biographical reflections of most CEOs and public officials, Firestone reveals missteps showing the lessons of resilience and how to detect dangerous mischief of others. "

—Jeffrey A. Sonnenfeld, Senior Associate Dean for Leadership
Studies, Lester Crown Professor of Leadership Practice,
Yale School of Management and author of *Firing
Back* and *The Hero's Farewell*

"*Even the Odds* is an eloquently written exploration of multiple facets of risk. By mixing risk management theory, business anecdotes, and her personal life story, Karen Firestone has created a highly readable book on a subject relevant to everyone."

—Lord Adair Turner, former Chairman of the UK Financial Services
Authority and author of *Between Debt and the Devil*

"Karen Firestone has produced a very thoughtful, articulate, and eminently readable book on how to think creatively about risk and deal with our uncertain world. I particularly enjoyed her anecdotes and vignettes on specific case studies of both personal and financial risk-taking, which include her blunt assessment of both successes and mistakes. She is persuasive in providing examples of how a more systematic assessment of risk might lead to better decisions and outcomes."

—Edward H. Ladd, Chairman Emeritus and CFA,
Standish Mellon Asset Management

"Even The Odds: Sensible Risk-Taking in Business, Investing, and Life is Karen Firestone's experience utilizing her personal courage and critical analytical sense to navigate through the riptides of the waters of billion dollar investments, take on the risks inherent in becoming CEO of an investment firm at the height of one of the nation's most historic financial collapses, and now help guide others through the uncertainties of their own risks."

—Peter Gammons, writer, journalist, and
analyst at the Major League Baseball Network

"Karen Firestone has brilliantly navigated market risk for many years. In **Even the Odds**, she offers us the gift of her clarity and pragmatism in assessing that risk. By showing us how to ask the right questions and unearth potential pitfalls, this book offers wisdom about how to pursue our dreams without losing our shirts—or our minds—in the process. . . . A smart, gutsy book, written by a smart, gutsy businesswoman."

—Robin Ely, Diane Doerge Wilson Professor of Business
Administration, Senior Associate Dean for Culture
and Community, Harvard Business School

EVEN
THE
ODDS

EVEN
THE
ODDS

SENSIBLE RISK-TAKING IN BUSINESS, INVESTING, AND LIFE

KAREN FIRESTONE

First published by Bibliomotion, Inc.
39 Harvard Street
Brookline, MA 02445
Tel: 617-934-2427
www.bibliomotion.com

Printed in the United States of America

Library of Congress Cataloging-in-Publication Data

Names: Firestone, Karen, author.
Title: Even the odds : sensible risk-taking in business, investing, and life
    / Karen Firestone.
Description: First Edition. | Brookline, MA : Bibliomotion, 2016.
Identifiers: LCCN 2016004362| ISBN 9781629560984 (hardback) | ISBN
    9781629560991 (ebook) | ISBN 9781629561004 (enhanced ebook)
Subjects: LCSH: Decision making. | Risk. | BISAC: BUSINESS & ECONOMICS /
    Decision-Making & Problem Solving.
Classification: LCC HD30.23 .F576 2016 | DDC 650.1—dc23
LC record available at http://lccn.loc.gov/2016004362

To David

CONTENTS

INTRODUCTION

I am a practitioner in the risk trade. You are too. Every day we face challenges that deal with exposure to uncertainties that range from benign to highly dangerous, from immaterial to very costly. We might nudge our car too aggressively into traffic at a busy intersection, interrupt a colleague in a meeting to make a controversial point, impulsively invest in a friend's start-up against our own better judgment, or decide to eat a loaded cheeseburger and secretly delight in the fact that we weren't offered a salad rather than fries.

The possible outcomes following these actions vary enormously, from a car accident and heartburn to financial debacle or a pleasant drive home, yet they illustrate the range of our daily risk-related experiences. Very often, we barely register the potential downside, and even when we should evaluate the situation carefully, our effort can be hopelessly inadequate.

My day job involves constant encounters with the unpredictable. My company invests money and manages the financial welfare of clients who trust us enough to pay for our expertise in making tough investment choices for them. We make our living by successfully analyzing risk and subverting the many factors that may bring our clientele tremendous financial pain. The practical focus of this book is directed toward constantly pursuing strategies of sensible risk-taking, to improve the outcomes of decisions and to add real value.

Other than a break to attend business school, I have spent my entire adult life in the investment business assessing risk. The stock market fascinated me from the time I was in fifth grade, when Mrs. Culhane had our class create a model portfolio that we followed and charted through the course of the year, keeping track of our gains and losses. IBM, Xerox, Kerr McGee, United Aircraft (now Technologies), and Eastman Kodak made up that 1967 portfolio. I sold United Aircraft and bought Flying Tiger and replaced Eastman Kodak with Avon. Those were the go-go years and we all made a killing—on paper. I suspect that Mrs. Culhane was playing the market actively herself.

I attended the Commonwealth School, a private high school in Boston, where I had a substantial scholarship thanks to the largesse of the school's founder and headmaster. His name was Charles Merrill, and his father, Charles E. Merrill Sr., had cofounded Merrill Lynch.[1] I asked Mr. Merrill to help me get a job at Merrill Lynch's office in Copley Square, close to the school. A devout liberal, Mr. Merrill put his head in his hands and shook it so vigorously that I was worried he was having a seizure. Finally, he looked up at me and said yes, he would arrange an interview with the branch manager, Bill Strott, with one important condition: I must promise never to become a "capitalist." Given that I didn't really understand the term at age sixteen, I agreed. (I have since apologized to Mr. Merrill for breaking the promise I made all those years ago.) The next day, there was a note for me on our bulletin board from Charlie Merrill. It said, "See Bill Strott at 3:30 p.m. tomorrow. WEAR A SKIRT!!!" I did, and Mr. Strott, who doubtless had little choice, hired me to do whatever menial tasks they needed done around the office. That was my first paid job in the investment business. I was in heaven.

Now, as the CEO of an investment firm I cofounded more than ten years ago, shortly before one of America's most severe financial crises, I understand the risks inherent in starting and building a new company. Before I started Aureus, I spent twenty-two years at Fidelity Investments, where I managed large growth funds with assets of more than $12 billion. During that experience, I grew to fully appreciate the risks in trading large equity positions and trying to outperform the market over a long period of time. My career also happened to coincide with raising four children, unquestionably adding another dimension of risk-related decisions to an already rich itinerary.

Even the Odds is about analyzing these various types of exposures by applying the four tenets of sensible risk-taking: right sizing, right timing, relying on knowledge and experience, and remaining skeptical of promises and forecasts. My experiences have forged these perspectives on risk evaluation, and they have helped me navigate some of the most severe challenges in my life, regardless of the arena in which those challenges appeared. Practical assessment of these tenets and their application is discussed through the real-life cases of people who have either mastered or neglected this approach to sensible risk-taking.

Even the Odds explores the individual parameters of each tenet, and then applies the tenets to the broader categories of business, investing, and life. Part 1 describes the properties and framework that characterize each tenet and looks at cases dominated by that principle. Part 2 considers the application of the tenets to business, including leaving one company to found another while building this new enterprise amidst major financial recession. Part 3 shows how I and other investors have used the risk-taking tenets to make judgments throughout our careers, along with cases where we wished we had paid closer attention to them. And part 4 describes evening the odds through the application of the tenets to one's personal life, through the lens of some difficult situations.

As we apply the four tenets of sensible risk-taking, we begin to recognize how frequently we encounter situations in which they are useful—we see how they can help us choose paths that will likely benefit us and avoid those that will probably bring harm. The consequences of failing to address risk can be devastating, ranging from losing money, a business, or our reputation to damaging our health and even losing our lives. Whether the decision is to start a new company, invest in a friend's enterprise, have a child, or go running in the dark, *Even the Odds* gives you a robust and easy-to-use framework for evaluating the risks and the rewards life throws our way every day.

The vignettes in this book are a mix of true stories of people I know, as well as composites of individuals whom I have come across through the years. All of them are designed to illustrate the role risk plays in our lives. When managed well, encountering risk can result in a very positive outcome. When misread or mismanaged, we may suffer an unmitigated disaster. Some of the stories you will read are also my own, and show how I've learned to approach risk.

From the time I divided a notebook page down the middle, to segment the plusses and minuses of attending a new school, I have consciously gravitated toward analyzing risk. I can recall cases when I have made sensible choices early in my life, such as choosing my job after business school and dating my future husband. Of course, there were also some severely deficient ones, including waiting too long to walk home in a huge blizzard, leaving me stranded in the underground subway system for hours. We learn from our successes and failures, and I have tried to offer insights from a life of evaluating risk taking—my own, and that of others I have observed.

PART 1

Sensible Risk-Taking

CHAPTER 1

Right Size Your Risk

Over the course of my career, risk has been my ever-present companion. Risk is well recognized and acknowledged, studied intensely from Wall Street to the halls of academia. Despite the contemplation and analysis, there remains a void in practical suggestions for how to handle mainstream risk-taking.

Too often, we ignore certain risks and disregard the possibility of unhappy consequences. The tenets I've outlined in *Even the Odds* are designed to improve decision making and help you avoid dire pitfalls. The allure of rewarding outcomes drives and often manipulates our perception of risk. Whether you are beginning to invest in emerging markets or are thinking of giving up your Wall Street job to teach, the results of major life changes are steeped in uncertainty, and the process of evaluating potential costs and benefits is daunting. Our pursuit of big rewards in all aspects of life can distort our ability to carefully consider a reasonable course of action.

My proficiency in balancing risks and rewards is perhaps my greatest core strength, and my experiences as an investor, a business owner, and a wife and mother of four have enabled me to distill principles of risk-taking that can be applied universally. These tenets—right sizing, right timing, relying on knowledge and experience, and remaining skeptical—have been effective in guiding my decisions both when I wrangled with international financial crises and when I had to choose a jogging partner. While the four principles are often interlaced in practice, one tenet frequently dominates the analysis, and it is helpful to isolate each as we discuss them.

The first tenet, right sizing, guides the scope of the risk you will incur. This risk might be monetary, emotional, or measured in time, effort, or energy. For example, there may be an oversized risk in taking a high-paying job that requires an hour drive each way if you tend to get sleepy at the wheel after thirty minutes. On the other hand, counseling your soccer-playing high school daughter to give the goalie position a chance is a reasonable bet: she might more easily make the varsity squad as a goalie, and she could always move back to defense. Individuals often have difficulty grasping how much may be at stake, even when they have a good sense of the potential reward or benefit they are seeking. We all have experienced problems with right sizing a risk. Following is one such problem that my firm faced a few years ago.

SETTING THE STRUCTURE

In 2005, I cofounded Aureus Asset Management, the firm for which I now serve as CEO, with my friend David Scudder. We created our company to offer families and individuals a means of investing using a style we call a "contemporary endowment model." Universities and nonprofit institutions had, for decades, invested across a wide range of assets, including domestic and international stocks, bonds, hedge funds, and liquid assets including real estate, private equity, and venture capital. Our goal was to do the same for individuals.

When making an investment, we carefully research each candidate and only take a position when we are convinced that a particular stock is a promising addition. We read all the financial information available on the company, review its SEC filings, and study the competitive landscape. Then we talk to the management, visit the headquarters, and build a detailed model of the future earnings and cash flow of the company. After all that, we discard at least 80 percent of the ideas because they do not offer enough reward given the cost.

We own no more than thirty-five to forty different stocks, so a new position would make up 2 or 3 percent of our clients' entire stock portfolios. After studying the benefits of diversification and attributes of concentration, as well as other factors, we determined early in our history that this was the right size for our positions. Each holding, though not particularly large, represents valuable "real estate" that we populate carefully.

TAKING THE PLUNGE

Although the return on our investment is the most important quality on which we are judged, there are sometimes additional factors and risks related to our clients' objectives. Halliburton represented such a case. In 2012, we began to study Halliburton, an oil services company whose past acts of environmental negligence had tarnished its reputation, even among conservative Americans who typically ignore such indictments. Former vice president Dick Cheney, who led the company from 1995 to 2000, staunchly denied every allegation of toxic dumping and violation of numerous federal and state regulations.[1]

Halliburton's alleged transgressions went far beyond dumping and polluting, however. On April 20, 2010, an explosion at the *Deepwater Horizon* drilling rig in the Gulf of Mexico killed eleven workers and injured sixteen. Halliburton had provided the cementing of the wall of the rig, which was owned by Transocean Drilling and operated by British Petroleum. Following the disaster, the stock prices of each of these participants, as well as all other players in the Gulf of Mexico energy sector, plummeted.

Our research team began to do some work on Halliburton, sensing that the worst news was behind it, though the stock had barely recovered since the spill. Though the company faced ongoing lawsuits related to dumping and transporting toxic chemicals, we sensed that Halliburton might be an attractive investment. The management sounded committed to more environmentally compliant behavior.

The stock was priced comparatively low relative to its industry peers on many financial metrics. The economy was recovering, and as it did, the price of oil was moving higher. We decided to buy Halliburton, paying between $27.99 and $42.07 per share over several months. We sized the position slightly over 2 percent for our accounts, a nod to the fact that the shares were volatile; we figured we could add more if the stock were to correct from that level. Fortunately, after fluctuating during the first half of 2012, Halliburton began a sustained uptrend.

LISTENING FOR RISK

Nearly two years after our investment in Halliburton, we were meeting with the investment committee of one of our largest nonprofit clients, a West Coast institution that owns and operates a beautiful nature reserve. The new chair of the committee explained that he had a problem with the trust owning stock in companies considered irresponsible and repeat environmental offenders, particularly in light of the organization's mission as steward of a forest and wildlife sanctuary.

We'd had a very strong relationship with the previous head of this group, who was a member of the family that established the gardens, but we knew little about the new chair. He had a specific problem with Halliburton in the portfolio. We outlined the rationale behind our ownership but had no success changing his mind. The investment committee promptly informed us that we needed to sell the stock before the end of the year. We had eight more months, which was plenty of time. We assured the committee that, of course, we would comply with their wishes.

Oil service stocks have a strong correlation with the price of oil; the higher the amount realized for each barrel drawn from the ground or ocean, the more exploration companies are willing to pay for its extraction. As the spring progressed, the price of oil moved higher. Sanctions against Russia because of its military actions in Ukraine and Crimea, and the crippling of several oil fields in beleaguered Libya and Iraq, helped constrain the estimated supply. Traders pushed the price of crude higher. By June, a barrel of West Texas intermediate crude sold for nearly $106. Other than the wild speculation of 2008, when crude skyrocketed in a summer spike to nearly $150 a barrel, this was close to an all-time high. In hindsight, this would have been the perfect time to eliminate the Halliburton stock, but neither my partners nor I felt strongly enough about an imminent price drop to spearhead the sale.

We were not thinking clearly about right sizing our risk, which was much more than the price of Halliburton stock. The true risk was in losing the account, which was one of our largest.

HEEDING THE WARNING

As the summer of 2014 progressed, oil prices drifted lower. The main culprit was the huge fracking-based incremental U.S. oil supply flooding the market. In addition, Middle East output remained steady. On the flip side, economic weakness in Europe depressed demand. Even if the Europeans were eager to stock up on oil, the strengthening dollar, in which oil is priced, was making each purchase costlier.

In early September of 2014, we again hosted the four-person nature preserve investment committee to our office for a review. The performance of the account had been very strong but the chair quickly raised the fact that Halliburton was still in the account. We noted that the mandate had been to sell the stock before the end of the year and we intended to do just that. I was able to interject that the stock was up 78 percent from the time of the purchase, but I heard muffled chuckling about how sometimes good outcomes result from bad decisions.

After the meeting, a few of us gathered in my office to discuss the risks in the portfolio with regard to the stocks, oil prices, and client retention. The United States and other world economies were in a recovery mode, which was positive for the commodity, but the supply picture was a major negative.

I then brought up the idea of selling Halliburton immediately to ensure we kept the nature preserve account, underscoring the true scope of our risk. The stock had fallen from a high of $73 in late July to the middle $60s. A couple of my partners argued that the stock might rally in the coming weeks, a reaction to extreme selling pressure in the energy sector. I agreed to call a friend who works in the oil industry to gauge his impression of the pricing environment, and then we would make a decision.

My contact in the oil industry assured me that oil would not possibly fall below the mid-$70s per barrel, which may not have been a meaningful drop to him, but it was more than 20 percent below where we were at the time.

ASSESSING THE OPTIONS

Reflecting on our possible courses of action, I described four potential outcomes to my partners. We knew that the committee did not want to own Halliburton, requiring a sale by year-end. Holding the stock was extremely risky. What if we held it and the stock went down? We would almost definitely lose the account, which generated an important fee.

If Halliburton climbed higher after we sold it, I was sure that no one on the committee would even notice. The same was true even if we held the stock and it advanced through year-end. At a 3 percent weight in the portfolio, there was virtually no upward move that could warrant retaining the position. The committee would not care. If we sold and the stock continued to decline, we would receive no credit, as they were the ones demanding that we divest the holding.

The answer was obvious to me: sell now. My partners agreed, and we sold the Halliburton stock in September for a 72 percent overall gain.

What happened? The price of West Texas crude continued to plummet, falling below $50 a barrel in early 2015, and Halliburton stock plunged to $37. We sold all our Halliburton holdings company wide before it reached that level, but wished we had acted as quickly for everyone as we did for the nature preserve. The most respected energy players were caught blindsided by this descent, although everyone with twenty-twenty hindsight admits that the signs were there.

This decision was not about predicting the stock price or the direction of crude oil, however, but about evaluating the size of the risk associated with not listening to the client's preference for environmentally responsible investing. The true scope of the risk was losing an important account; the clock was ticking, we knew the client's wishes, and we were all skeptical about the experts' opinions on oil prices. Once we analyzed the decision carefully, we knew that we had no option other than to sell the stock. Upon informing the committee we had sold the Halliburton, we received little more acknowledgment than "Good." That response was far better than hearing, "You're fired," a distinct possibility if we failed to right size the risk.

BENEATH THE RADAR

I would never call myself a daredevil or characterize myself as personally reckless in any meaningful way. I might jaywalk in downtown Boston, but only when it would be impossible for anyone to drive fast enough to hurt me or when there are no cars in sight. I have never driven when I am intoxicated, not only because I don't really like to drink, but also because I don't want to risk getting caught, losing my license, or causing an accident. I would never swim at a beach if someone told me he had spotted a great white shark the day before, and I canceled a plan to learn to skydive when two people died at the facility where I was going to take lessons.

However, I did go to work on the day of the lockdown in the aftermath of the Boston Marathon bombing. That chilling event, on the afternoon of April 15, 2013, shocked everyone in the city of Boston and beyond. It is amazing and horrifying to contemplate the enormous risk, which these runners were not aware of. Around two o'clock on the afternoon of the marathon, I had driven across Commonwealth Avenue, one of the main thoroughfares on which the race is run, on my way from work to a funeral. I saw the racers and felt slightly, though not very, jealous.

Growing up, I lived a few blocks from the marathon route. Every year on Patriots' Day, a state holiday in Massachusetts, my mother and I would walk to Cleveland Circle to see the runners turn from Chestnut Hill Avenue onto Beacon Street for the final few miles of their journey. I have also run the Boston Marathon and, as anyone who has run a marathon can tell you, it's exhilarating but, man, it's not easy. As a friend of mine who has run about thirty marathons says, if you finish, you beat all those good runners who sat out the race that day.

On that gorgeous April afternoon, two bombs went off within seconds of each other at 2:49 p.m., killing three people and injuring 264. At the memorial service I was attending that afternoon, people started getting text messages from friends and family asking if they were okay. The whole city was in a state of shock and the suspects remained at large for several days.

Finally, in the early evening of Thursday, April 18, FBI Special Agent Richard DesLauriers and Carmen Ortiz, the United States Attorney for Massachusetts, held a press conference and reported that they had identified two suspects whom they believed had set off the bombs. As Agent DesLauriers spoke, a video of the two young suspects moving across the screen played eerily, over and over. His voice calmly stated that the suspects were likely armed and dangerous. Soon after the video aired, the tip line began to ring.

Friday I went to my 6:15 a.m. spin class, but while changing after class in the locker room, a staff member ran in to tell us that the gym was closing, we needed to leave, and it had something to do with the marathon bombing.

I got in my car and listened to a radio broadcast that said the suspects had killed an MIT campus policeman the night before, then engaged in a shootout with the police in Watertown, a city adjacent to Boston on the northwest side. One suspect was killed and the other had escaped, so the authorities were going door to door in Watertown. Because of the urgency of the search, Governor Deval Patrick requested that citizens in adjoining cities and towns "shelter in place" for the day.

Despite the official warning, I decided to go in to my office, which is five or six miles from Watertown. I estimated that the risk of being injured was no greater than on any other day, and probably less because there were fewer cars on the road. I likewise decided I would not impede the investigation from such a distance. I evaluated the size of the risk to me and to other individuals as extremely small. So, I drove to work believing that the scope of potential danger to me or caused by me would be minute. Of course, if every other commuter had reached a similar conclusion, the roads would have been packed; on the other hand, most people offered a day off are very happy to take it.

There was also another factor that contributed to my decision. Jeremy Goldsmith,* a client prospect and one of the city's most successful lawyers, had set up an appointment for that day and had already confirmed. Jeremy's office was only a block away from mine. Something made me think that Jeremy would also go to work that day, and I was loath to e-mail him that I was staying home.

If he were in Boston and we met, I thought—perhaps optimistically—that

---

* Jeremy Goldsmith is a pseudonym.

my company had a strong chance of winning the account. When I arrived at my desk, I e-mailed my colleagues that they should comply with the governor's wishes and stay home, although a couple of people biked in anyway. I wrote to Jeremy to tell him that I was in the office, and he told me, as I had suspected, that he was in that day as well.

He arrived right on time, and we discussed, of course, the tragic nature of the bombing and its aftermath. He explained that he did not think that his presence on the Mass Pike would have any effect on the investigation and he found the deserted weekday streets an interesting phenomenon. The police did capture Dzhokhar Tsarnaev, bleeding from shotgun wounds, in a boat perched in a Watertown backyard, and Jeremy hired us. Would he have done so if I had rescheduled the appointment for another day? Of course, it is impossible to know, but there is a risk that he would have met and selected another investment advisor in the meantime.

Did I put myself in danger that day by coming into the office? I don't think so. I do know that I would make the same decision today. Plus, I would never have just stayed in my house all day, and if I ended up playing lousy golf, I would have been really annoyed.

Although this case of right sizing is very different from the Halliburton example, both illustrate the framework of applying the principle of right sizing to a situation where the total risk may be greater than it appears at first glance. It is often difficult in the heat of an emotional or pressured moment to grasp the true scope of the risk, which is exactly why we should, if the situation allows, calmly review the range of options, their costs, and their payoffs.

Sometimes, the risk may be less than initially presented, as with the Boston Marathon aftermath and my own physical danger. Frequently, the payoff becomes clear only after we analyze our options fully. Right sizing helps us think through the residual effects our decisions may have, such as losing or retaining a client, which may have little to do with the investment returns we generally focus on in my industry. Once we think in terms of sensible risk-taking, the various exposures become more obvious and easier to distinguish.

CHAPTER 2

Right Time Your Risk

The timing we use in confronting risk is often critical. For example, you do not want to set out on a fishing trip when the weather report warns of thunderstorms. Releasing a new film is always an uncertain endeavor, but if you drop a low-budget family film the same weekend the latest *Star Wars* movie hits the theaters, you are asking for trouble. If there are three houses on your street for sale, it might make sense to wait before listing your own, as a fourth on the market might cause potential buyers to question why so many homeowners are leaving that particular location.

One of the four tenets of sensible risk-taking is right timing, which is the process of evaluating how risk will change based on exactly when we take action.

Right timing rises in importance when people, markets, trends, and environments are changing and the specific move we are considering will be helped or hurt by our timing. You might not want to open a new ski store in July or an ice cream shop in December, for example. If you are a young political operative, you might consider starting your own political consulting firm a couple of years before a presidential election, when numerous offices will be up for grabs. Any later, and the timing will be inauspicious. In addition to timing related to business conditions or other outside influences, there are matters of timing related to your personal situation. Your individual experience, training, age, or attitudes may render confronting a challenge at a particular time right or wrong.

MAKING THE PITCH

Anytime we seek to transform our role within an organization, we face career uncertainty, and that is exactly what I did in 2004. I found myself staring at the inside of the elevator at 82 Devonshire Street, the site of Fidelity's former headquarters, on my way to the fifth-floor executive suite. I disembarked, turned the corner, and saw the beautiful Japanese garden that our chairman, Ned Johnson, had planted years before.

I was there to see Roger Servison, one of the highest-ranking and longest-tenured managers within Fidelity, which was well known for the revolving door of top administrators surrounding Mr. Johnson. Roger was an anomaly at Fidelity in that he cared deeply about his attire and always wore a bow tie, well-polished loafers, and well-made shirts. He was also soft spoken and calm, two qualities in scarce supply among my stock-picking colleagues. My mission was to convince him that I had a strong concept for a new division inside the company, and that I could spearhead the new group.

Inside Roger's office, I took a deep breath and launched into my pitch. Wouldn't it be a great idea, I said, since we offered limited personalized investment advice, if I became the portfolio manager for our fifty largest individual clients? Instead of making decisions on their own, they would have a highly trained and experienced professional managing their money.

I was a senior fund manager requesting that Fidelity create a job that I wanted. That was certainly bold and perhaps foolish, but I had determined that the time was right and that this was a role that both fit my skills and would help my employer move into a new market. My current assignment was managing several stock funds, the largest being Destiny 1 Fund, which I had taken over in 1998 when its long-time manager, George Vanderheiden, decided to turn over the fund and chose me as his successor.

Each mutual fund at Fidelity had one manager who took all the credit for good performance and all the blame when results turned south. In 2004, when I was in my late forties, I was not certain I had the stamina for another ten years running $12 billion. Essentially, I wanted to create a new product line at Fidelity, not a new fund—I was advocating for a portfolio advisory division that would service our very wealthy individual clients, who might otherwise move their assets to find that service.

Roger asked me to elaborate on my proposal. If there were fifty Fidelity clients with $100 million each, I would be managing $5 billion. In his thoughtful manner, he pointed out that I now was responsible for more than twice that much money, so why would the company favor this change? I could feel the air leak from my popped balloon. I had not anticipated that question, and it was a good one.

Just because I had outlined my agenda did not mean that Roger Servison and the company would share my perspective. In fact, I barely considered my potential move from Fidelity's point of view, which included the very real risk that moving me off my product line would be a mistake. My new efforts would generate lower fees because of the smaller assets under my care, the initiative could take years to ramp up, and I had very little experience with client service, which would likely be a major component of my job. Why would Fidelity want to mess with a winning approach?

I stood up, thanked Roger for his time, shook his hand, and left the office. On my way down the elevator, out the front door, and down the street to my office, I realized that, in my enthusiasm for my own idea, I had totally blown my opportunity to make a strong case for myself.

It was at that moment that I began to consider the idea of not just leaving my current position but of leaving the company where I had spent nearly half my life, and starting something new. I had made a step in a direction, and perhaps I should keep walking while I explored the nature of the risks and returns implied.

Right timing seemed to be a dominant factor in the decision I was about to make, as I reviewed the reasons I wanted a change. I was seven years into the job to which I had always aspired, and I was growing restless.

GIVING UP A LOT

I understood that if I were to go into business for myself, I would be giving up a great deal. At the time, my role as one of the managers of a large U.S. mutual fund was among the most coveted at the company; it might have been one of the best in the entire investment management industry. In 2004, Fidelity Investments was the most successful fund company in the world, with assets of more than $1 trillion.[1] As was true of all the Fidelity portfolio managers at the time, I made all the purchase and sale decisions for the assets in my fund, subsequently taking all the credit or blame, which was definitely an intense experience.

In 2004, Jennifer Uhrig and I were the only two women who managed large U.S. stock funds that invested across all industries, although we had two talented female colleagues who gave up their funds to follow other pursuits. My funds were Destiny 1 Fund, Large Cap Fund, and several others, sold through different sales forces to different markets.

I had arrived at Fidelity fresh from Harvard Business School in June of 1983. A female friend in the investment business warned me not to take the job, because Fidelity would surely chew me up and spit me out. That sounded like the perfect environment for me: the culture seemed hard charging, the company hired analysts with a mix of backgrounds and genders, and I felt up to the challenge.

I discovered that I was pregnant with twins before graduating from business school, and, in a rare twist of career fate, I was offered a choice role as an assistant fund manager on Magellan Fund, run by the legendary Peter Lynch. Normally, new MBAs are assigned as analysts following an industry group, but Peter needed some additional help, and though I would be taking some time off, I already had four years of investment experience. I worked for Peter until the birth of my twins and through their first year, and then assumed coverage of my first industry groups.

Over the years, I followed many industries as an analyst, sector fund manager, and group head for health care. I also had two more children along the way, so by age thirty I had four kids under four years old. Very tiring, to say the least.

As a young woman, I always imagined that my career would be long and fulfilling, but I didn't realize that a working mother raising four children needs to develop patience about the speed of her career. Most of my peers, male and female, had no children, fewer children, or a spouse whose full-time job was caring for the house and family.

Many of my male colleagues advanced much more quickly than I did, but I did not complain. Debating the fairness of my situation was irrelevant; I knew that if I kept studying companies and proving my value as an investor, I would be rewarded. In 1997, after fourteen years at Fidelity, I was finally promoted to manage my first portfolio that could own stocks in all industries.

Seven years later, in 2004, there were twenty to twenty-five people at the firm who managed stock mutual funds with assets at the same size or larger than mine. Each of us was under considerable pressure to beat our benchmark, whether it was the S&P 500, a mid-cap, or an overseas index. In exchange, we were highly compensated. The leading mutual fund institutions were amazingly profitable. Just one fund with assets of $10 billion charging three-quarters of 1 percent generated $75 million annually.

THE RIGHT PLACE FOR THE TIME

The explosion in the 401(k) market was the greatest thing that ever happened to firms like Fidelity, which quickly perfected the art of selling a suite of fund offerings to every Fortune 500 company.

As the market moved higher through most of the 1980s and '90s, employees—with their newfound control over their own retirement assets—increasingly selected stock mutual funds for this exposure. Fidelity offered them an incredible array of products. Funds were named for the size of the market value of the stocks held, such as Large Cap, Mid Cap, and Small Cap; the investment concept underlying the fund, including Growth Company, Blue Chip, Balanced, and Value. And, of course, there were those names that imply wealth, clever investing, and a better future: Magellan, Contrafund, and Destiny.

As the assets poured into Fidelity funds, the people who managed the large, diversified stock funds became our industry's equivalent of rock stars. Fidelity started a car service, Boston Coach, which had as its primary function ferrying fund managers to and from Logan Airport. We were awarded stock each year, assuming that our fund was keeping up with the benchmark, and the assets under our control grew and grew. Wall Street salespeople tripped over one another to host fund managers at concerts and sporting events.

On any given day, thirty to forty company managements came through our offices to meet with, and hopefully impress, the analyst responsible for providing in-depth coverage and analysis of the stock, and with the fund managers who currently owned the equity or might buy it in the future. Public corporations heralded our ownership the same way soap makers might covet the Good Housekeeping Seal of Approval.

WHY JUMP SHIP NOW?

A couple of years before speaking to Roger Servison, I had observed that most of the generation of fund managers ahead of me seemed to reach a point where they became averse to the daily pressure to outperform the market, or they simply wanted to have a less frenetic lifestyle. At that point, they retired from their funds. While I was very happy in my current position, I could imagine that I might reach that threshold five years into the future.

It was the right time for a change because I was, for the first time, interested in something new and different. I wanted to keep working full time in the investment business and had not contemplated working for a different company. I liked my idea—even if Roger didn't—so why not pursue it outside of Fidelity? Of course, as with all new enterprises, there would be many risks, but, again, the timing seemed right.

Not only did I feel ready for a change in some of my workplace functions, but it was the right time given my responsibilities outside the office. By this time, the youngest of our children was eighteen years old, which meant that all of our children would be in college or beyond within a year. Of course, as most couples today know, there is the occasional fledgling who returns to the empty nest, but offspring that old do not need to be driven to multiple activities, require help with school projects, or involve a lot of extra cooking.

Another factor in right timing my move was that I was financially secure after more than two decades at a successful company where I had been well compensated. Fidelity is a private company, with majority ownership by the Johnson family and minority ownership by a relatively small number of fund managers, analysts, and other professionals. I was lucky enough to have been a shareholder in Fidelity since close to my start date, and that stock, which I would need to sell back upon my departure, was worth a considerable amount.

I knew that I had the investment ability and knowledge to manage assets inside or outside Fidelity, but I also believed that the twenty-two years during which I had worked full time while raising my children had helped hone key organizational skills that would come in very handy as I built and managed a start-up.

Finally, I was in my late forties, and if I was going to leave my job to create a new enterprise, the time was right to take that leap. There were multitudes of questions to be answered—such as whether I would do this on my own or with partners, what products or services my company would offer, and who would hire me—but taking the step at this time was the primary decision I had to make.

It was the right time to leave Fidelity. I had evaluated the factors in my life that would pertain to leaving my wonderful, high-paying job, and I was ready and prepared to start a business. Thus began my next journey—into entrepreneurship—where I would need to trust my long experience and hard-won skills.

CHAPTER 3

Rely on Knowledge, Skills, and Experience

No one would or should think of signing up for an expedition to summit Mt. Everest without having done some serious climbing. People who become building contractors have usually worked or trained as carpenters or in other aspects of construction before they take on their new roles. New ad agencies, law firms, and retail establishments spring from roots in similarly focused organizations.

The third tenet of sensible risk-taking is to rely on knowledge, skills, and experience. This means that consistently applying skills we have honed over years of a sustained career or continuous practice will help ensure a favorable outcome. My background was investing, so it was no surprise that my new venture was an investment company. When my friend Patty Bright—a banker who took fifteen years off to be a stay-at-home mom—wanted to reenter the work force, she became co-owner of a knitting shop because she is an incredible knitter and has the financial understanding required to manage the business. Although she had never worked professionally in the knitting or crafts field, she had considerable experience. Sticking with what we know is a definite way to even the odds.

Of course, there are many situations where we need to develop new competencies that we lack; in these cases, we can devote the time and effort necessary to acquire those skills ourselves, partner with someone who already has them, or purchase them. When my partners and I started our business, none of us knew much about compliance, an important requirement at any financial services firm. I became enough of an expert at our inception to know the right questions to ask our attorney and to navigate the many regulations and complete filings with the Securities and Exchange Commission.

Over my lifetime, I have seen many people deviate from their strengths with frustrating results. We face enough hurdles in our business, investing, and personal lives that adding a lack of understanding of the particular challenges will not increase the chance of success. Of course, environments change, and these changes may demand that our style and approach evolve as well. In that case, we can often successfully redirect our core knowledge and competencies.

SHIFTING JEWELS

An antique jewelry store in Geneva's venerable shopping district may not inspire the image of a rapidly changing business environment, but images can be deceiving. Roberto Conti,* who attended college in the United States, always knew he would return to Geneva to join his father, Eduardo, in the family business. For generations, Conti Jewelers had served a global clientele from a beautiful and tasteful store set in an eighteenth-century former manor house in the center of the city. The jewelry industry is one of the oldest on the planet. Traditionally, women wore the pieces, men bought them, and merchants concentrated on selling to the

---

* Roberto Conti, Conti Jewelers, and related names are pseudonyms.

wealthy in their vicinity rather than displaying their products universally. That tradition, however, was beginning to shift.

Conti specialized in antique jewelry—which Roberto confidentially refers to as "used"—and major signed pieces that they bought from clients or other dealers or at auctions. But they also sold modern gold bracelets and pieces by contemporary designers. Decades ago, Roberto and his father realized that the single store on Rue du Marché wasn't sufficient to generate the type of income they desired. Eduardo had dabbled in buying and selling paintings, at times acquiring some fantastic canvases from estates from which they were buying jewelry, but this effort was fraught with the risk of fakes and fraud, both of which they had encountered. Not only did fine paintings require considerable capital that might be employed elsewhere, but Roberto believed that sustainable strength in this field stretched too far from their skill set.

He considered opening a few Conti Jewelers stores in other European cities and manufacturing their own branded line of jewelry, but rejected both ideas because of the enormous cost, effort, and, in his opinion, low probability of success. In addition, Roberto and Eduardo valued their lifestyle, including leisurely lunches, as one of the key benefits of their profession, and neither wanted to work longer hours. Their store rarely stayed open past seven, with a break, of course, for lunch, but it was open six days a week most of the year.

The Internet was also changing the nature of their business. Buyers could scour websites for auction houses, high-end dealers, and retail establishments anywhere on the globe. Sellers of rare jewelry pieces in their own Swiss market could easily contact someone in New York who would fly over to examine and potentially buy a lot on which the Contis would historically have had the first showing.

Roberto needed to direct the business in a way that optimized their deep knowledge of rare items within this modern world of instantaneous digital information, and which focused on the concentration of wealth in the hands of individuals whose purchases were not constrained by their home base. He determined that if they were going to take on more risk, they should stick with what they knew best: valuing, buying, and selling large, important stones and designed pieces of antique jewelry. They had opportunities to purchase such lots either on their own or in partnerships with other dealers across Europe or from the United States. The Contis would be more aggressive about making sure that their colleagues in the business understood that they had available capital, unlike many of their competitors, and they were interested in such investments.

The challenge was to find worthy pieces on which they could make a decent profit. The risks of investing large sums in sizable objects were that their capital was tied up for long periods and that they could misjudge the value and overpay. If they used discipline in applying their knowledge and avoided impulsive purchases, they could expand their business successfully.

Roberto told his associates in the jewelry business that he was interested in participating in the purchase of large pieces. Conti Jewelers was known to be well capitalized, which Roberto and Eduardo knew enhanced their reputation as reliable partners.

THE DISCOVERY AND PURCHASE

In 2007, a good friend in Milan called the Contis to say that they had a once-in-a-lifetime opportunity—a phrase that tends to be overused by jewelers and other enthusiastic merchants—to acquire a very rare twenty-six-carat blue diamond.

Not only was the size unusual for a quality diamond, but the color rendered it particularly appealing for the type of venture Roberto and Eduardo sought beyond the walls of their store. There were two potential problems. The first was that the stone had no certificate from a reputable rating agency, such as the Gemological Institute of America (GIA), attesting to its quality, and the second was that the owners would not release the stone until after it was paid for in full. Without a certificate, the buyers risked overpaying for a blue diamond that could end up being chemically or artificially treated, receive a poor designation from the GIA, or both. These were serious and expensive concerns.

Roberto and two potential partners viewed the stone in Milan and believed they were in the presence of an extremely rare precious gem that was untreated and worthy of a "vivid" GIA rating. They had a wealth of knowledge of colored stones among the three of them; they knew that other potential buyers, which could include some of the most celebrated in the business, would be worried about the lack of certification and either bid very low or not at all; and they understood that even if they received the best classification possible, there were only a handful of potential clients in the world for such an important jewel.

Together they determined a price that they felt would not expose Conti Jewelers to collapse if the market for large stones did not appreciate. While they could end up holding this diamond for years, they understood that this was a perennial challenge in their business. They bid well under $1 million a carat, but much higher than another bidding group whose offer underscored the lack of a certificate. Roberto believed the blue diamond could fetch several times their cost.

The offer was accepted, the partners celebrated the purchase in Milan, and then one of them accompanied the diamond to New York for the GIA appraisal. The wait was uncomfortable. When the institute finally completed its review, the blue diamond received the best rating: "vivid," which designates a stone that is not dark, not light, but just right. Roberto and his father were both relieved and gratified by the institute's findings. Applying their extensive experience and judgment in analyzing the diamond had been a key element in reducing the risk that they were overpaying.

THE SALE

The selling process was now underway. In 2007, world stock markets were high, billionaires were in abundant supply, and the partners felt very comfortable that they would end the year with a large profit in hand. They passed on one offer as inadequate, although it far surpassed the amount they had paid. The calendar rolled into 2008 and they rejected another offer. Roberto began to worry about the level of capital the Contis had invested in that one stone, its lack of liquidity, and the possibility that they were being too greedy. He did not want to "wrong time" this endeavor by losing a huge sale and stressing the company's balance sheet.

Then, to their incredible bad luck, the global markets collapsed in tandem. There were no inquiries about the blue diamond for well over a year. Roberto was a nervous wreck. Eduardo had become very sick and Roberto was already distressed about his father's health and the overall state of the business.

In 2010, one of the partners received a call that the head of state of a Middle Eastern country wanted to see the stone. Roberto and one of his colleagues flew with the merchandise and waited in their hotel to be summoned. There was no guarantee that they would be safe. In fact, if the police or the military arrested them and demanded they turn over the diamond, they would have no choice—a risk that they honestly did not anticipate when they made the purchase. Roberto and his partners had done the best due diligence on the client that they could, using whatever contacts they had in the Middle East without drawing attention to a very private transaction. This could be the buyer for the biggest deal of their lives.

They were thrilled that the customer loved the stone and had agreed, after some negotiation, to the price the partners had determined would be acceptable. Roberto left for Geneva with a check and passport in hand. The bet paid off fantastically, but it took much longer and caused more consternation along the way than Roberto had ever imagined. Eduardo, however, never saw the conclusion of their new venture; he had died the year before, but told Roberto that he trusted him to complete the sale successfully.

The Conti example showcases how a long-standing family business used accumulated knowledge and skills to reinvigorate its business by gaining a place at the table among the dealers engaged in the highest order or purchases and sales in their field.

We all have accumulated skills and inherent talents that influence our careers and personal lives. Trusting and remaining true to the insights informed by that knowledge is a key component to sensible risk-taking. Also, we need to understand that we can acquire new skills as environments change and we can partner with colleagues who complement our own background.

In the case of the Contis, the size of the risk and the potential reward were great, the timing was the present, and their knowledge was deep. However, sometimes the best analysis and planning benefit from a little luck. If the eventual customer had passed on the deal, the partners may have needed to wait several years for another buyer. Fortunately, luck was on their side. Still, relying on knowledge as a foundation of risk-taking is essential, whether or not you get that extra boost.

CHAPTER 4

Maintain Your Skepticism

It is easy to find comfort in a beautifully composed set of projections on a detailed spreadsheet, but we should never mistake a column of numbers for the truth. The fourth tenet of sensible risk-taking is maintaining skepticism of projections, forecasts, and promises that might inspire a false sense of confidence. Applying appropriate skepticism means being unafraid to raise questions, taking your time while you come to a conclusion, and walking away if you cannot become comfortable with the response.

Pay a visit to a local car dealership on a Saturday and you can witness some powerful cases of suggestion and sales seduction at work. We are all susceptible to a great sales pitch, particularly when the item is something we really want. Our consumer culture ensures that we are bombarded with advertisements every day. While many people acknowledge the pervasiveness of marketing and the way it influences our decisions, it takes effort to remain dutifully skeptical. Rather than focus on emotion, we need to step back and reevaluate the choice sensibly.

In many cases, describing the potential purchase or concept to a trusted friend or family member can be helpful, just as a sanity check. Often, the process of recounting the benefits of a deal that's too good to be true can reveal its shortcomings. Also, another person's perspective may help crystallize unanswered questions about the idea. If the deal is genuinely strong, it will pass further inquiry, but if the price is too high, the emotional cost excessive, or the valuation unrealistic, some cynicism is necessary.

To peruse an income projection, with its equally sized and shaded numbers and letters, is to be lulled into a false sense of security. There are no gradations of font size or tone to clue us that some numbers are vastly more credible than others. I have always wondered why the numbers for "interest expense" on a spreadsheet, which would be available years in advance, are not presented in a much darker shade than the line for licensing software revenue, which is considerably harder to predict.

Lack of skepticism is a sin in my business. It is also toxic. If you are gullible, you deserve to lose money; it's as simple as that. To be successful as a stock picker, you must have the unnatural combination of strong cynicism and a dogged commitment to what you believe.

Over the years, I have sat through many meetings with corporate managements where the thought "You've got to be kidding" has run through my mind so loudly that I almost needed to cover my mouth. This type of skepticism would have been very helpful in the case study that follows.

TRUST

Sometimes, competent and intelligent people allow themselves to sink into tremendously risky situations. They fail to understand the scope of their risk and fall hostage to unconditional faith.

Dean Henderson* was one of those people. He was an ophthalmologist

---

*Dean Henderson is a pseudonym.

originally from Lincoln, Nebraska, who made his way east for education, married Lynne, a beautiful Texan, had three gorgeous children, and became a highly regarded member of their Episcopal church. The only clue to a daredevil streak was the fact that Dean had been a star diver on the Princeton swim team. As someone who swam on her college team, and had the chance to dive off the ten-meter diving platform on many occasions, I found that one belly flop was enough to scare me out of the next.

Dean and a couple of his friends from medical school formed a practice in 1971 called Vision Health and Surgical Services.* They attracted several other eye doctors, and their practice grew steadily. Several of them were enamored with entrepreneurial ideas, and at first the ventures they invested in were related to their profession, such as a retinal scope that could see behind a patient's eyes. Dean was a huge believer in these exciting ventures, even as the opportunities moved far afield of eye therapy.

One of these start-ups, which originated with a friend of one of Dean's partners, was a mortgage banking company whose primary customers lacked the credit scores to qualify for traditional home loans. The second enterprise bought faltering radio stations with the intention of turning them around. The fact that Dean and his fellow ophthalmologists had no previous experience in these other businesses did not seem to raise a red flag.

By the recession of 1991, both the mortgage banking and the radio businesses had gone bankrupt. Despite losing millions, the doctors were running a very successful practice, led by cataract surgery—an increasingly common treatment for glaucoma and a hugely profitable procedure for eye surgeons. Although the core business was performing extremely well and all the partners were earning strong salaries, one of the partners had another investment that he sold hard to Dean.

---

*Vision Health and Surgical Services is a pseudonym.

UNDERMINING CONDITIONS

Dean's partner was pushing a company called Care Codes.* The concept seemed simple: relieve doctors of the headache of compiling the forms and coding the procedures that Medicare now required before releasing payments to providers. Not only did Vision Health need a system like this, but, as one of the owners, it would capitalize on the entire industry's need for this service. Several of the partners thought it was a fantastic idea.

Dean conceded to his colleagues again, committing the firm's capital to a venture about which he knew very little. He suspended any cynicism about the concept before agreeing to this costly suggestion. Although Dean was the CEO of Vision Health and its busiest eye surgeon, he paid little attention to the firm's back office, relinquishing that role to one of the other team members.

All too often, people allow themselves to be drawn into situations of extreme risk that violate sensible risk-taking principles because they are blinded by their unconditional trust in others' abilities. As with any payments system, Medicare attracts abusers, many of whom have been successful. In addition to streamlining the reimbursement by the federal government for each diagnostic test and medical procedure, Care Codes and other services could facilitate payment of a test or surgery that never took place. Attorneys general around the country began to investigate cases first brought to their attention by Medicare investigators and whistleblowers within practitioners' offices.

The U.S. General Accounting Office (GAO) estimated in 1997 that Medicare fraud was costing the government at least $20 billion a year.[1] The FBI, Department of Justice, and every conceivable law enforcement agency tried to combat this crime epidemic, which was labeled the "Crisis of the 1990s." As just one example, a California ophthalmologist was

---

*Care Codes is a pseudonym.

found guilty of netting $15.5 million from Medicare for either unnecessary or nonexistent cataract and eyelid surgeries.[2]

Lynne isn't sure when Dean learned that the attorney general's office was looking into Vision Health's association with Care Codes and the company's billing records, because he may have kept that news from her for months. Dean was called to testify numerous times in the early 1990s before Massachusetts Attorney General Scott Harshbarger and his staff.

The government charged that Care Codes had assisted its physician clients in defrauding Medicare by overstating the services they were providing. Vision Health was allegedly both an equity owner in the abusive company con and also a participant in overbilling. What Dean thought was a legitimate cost-saving and time-saving software system was likely involved in scam artistry. One of the partners who had been a huge advocate for Care Codes left the medical practice, leaving Dean to take the heat as the fall guy at the state hearings.

Vision Health was not found guilty of any criminal intent to defraud the government, but by 1994 the practice had paid millions in settlement costs and legal fees. The experience, as one might expect, scarred Dean for life. He became despondent, reclusive outside of work, and paranoid about the government or any regulatory authority.

NAIVETÉ RESURRECTED

Dean feared that with the turn of the year 2000, the software problem known as Y2K would decimate global banking systems; the fact that this didn't occur was little consolation. He began to see conspiracies everywhere—the stock market collapse in 2000 was part of a plot to erase private savings, and the attack on the World Trade Center was the beginning of the end of democracy, if not civilization. Dean saw risk everywhere, focusing his undivided attention on how to avoid it.

He began to follow economist Chris Martenson, the guru of

doomsday preppers. Martenson's website, Peak Prosperity, uses the theme "Insights for Prospering as Our World Changes,"[3] but the underlying message is that the world is disintegrating and the reader needs to be prepared. The articles and photographs the company publishes suggest imminent catastrophe, among them "The Fatal Flaw of Centrally Issued Money," "Ocean Acidification: An Ecological Nightmare," and features about the coming nuclear warfare between Russia and the United States, with titles like "Special Report: Is It Time to Prepare For War?"[4] Dean traveled to hear Martenson speak several times, subscribed to his newsletters, and began to organize his life around imminent Armageddon.

As he approached retirement and his seventieth birthday, a decade after 9/11, Dean convinced Lynne to buy a five-hundred-acre farm in southern New Hampshire, hopefully far enough from urban centers to avoid destruction from a nuclear warhead. They took classes in sustainable farming to prepare for their move to the country when he retired from Vision Health. Dean arranged to work part time at an ophthalmology practice in a nearby town once he was fully disengaged from Vision Health.

Unfortunately, that never happened. Three weeks before they were to begin moving out of their home in Brookline, Massachusetts, Dean suffered a massive stroke. I had seen him very close to that date— looking healthy and extremely excited to show me photos of the farm and describe what he and Lynne had been learning in their farm management course. He died a few days after the stroke.

WHERE SKEPTICISM WOULD HAVE HELPED

In the weeks and months following Dean's death, Lynne began to unravel the extreme depths of his paranoia. He had cashed out his IRA, along with his insurance policies, and invested all the money in gold bars at about $1,900 per ounce, close to its record price. When Lynne tried to sell the position, the price of gold had fallen 26 percent from Dean's cost. She also discovered that the storage facility where the gold was held had been charging egregious fees. Dean's equity in Vision Health was worth much less than she anticipated because Dean had felt obliged to pay a disproportionately larger percentage of the settlement with the government out of his own pocket. To cover the estate taxes, Lynne had to sell the New Hampshire farm at a loss.

How did all this happen? Dean was too trusting of charismatic people, setting aside any healthy skepticism he may have felt and letting their promises and rhetoric cloud and corrupt his judgment. He allowed the practice to invest the partnership's money in ventures about which Dean knew very little until it was too late. After the Medicare investigation finally ended, Dean, his self-respect and confidence shattered, lost all regard for traditional institutions. He failed to accurately assess the world around him, choosing instead to follow a few isolated opinions. Dean never told Lynne about his decision to place an excessive amount of his assets into gold or the fact that he had closed his retirement account and cashed in his life insurance policy.

Dean may have felt that he was reducing his family's risk by circumventing the financial and governmental bureaucracies in which he had lost all faith, but he was adding tremendous exposure in other areas: with regard to the price of gold and farmland in New Hampshire, for example. He failed to recognize the scope of the risk he was taking with his family's future financial well-being. He needed a reality check but refused to shake his determination to avoid the "system" that had failed him.

Dean's story sadly illustrates how the illusion of risk control can mask true danger. In the end, Dean could not even confide in his wife or family members, a clear sign that he was exposing them to abundant risk.

If you cannot admit to your spouse that you are making a huge investment, you need to think further about your involvement and why you are afraid to discuss it. In Dean's case, running through each aspect of sensible risk-taking would have helped him address the size of the commitments he was making, the timing, and what he knew or did not know about each of them—and it would have helped him apply some healthy skepticism to others' promises and predictions.

Perhaps if Dean had shared his paranoia with his family, he might have avoided some of the dangerous pitfalls, such as the large bet on gold, and not been under so much stress when the price collapsed. We will never know, as Dean, unfortunately, never tried any of these logical steps.

We know that projections and forecasts, particularly those described in impressive-looking reports or by articulate proponents, inspire a false sense of confidence by inhibiting our natural skepticism. Never be afraid to ask questions about claims that seem somewhat unlikely at best or outlandish at worst. Consider the source of the information, what that person has to gain by convincing you, and whether he can be trusted. If you are inclined to move ahead with a plan that is costly, whether in money, effort, or time, describe the premise to a trusted friend or family member—that might just illuminate some deficiencies that had eluded you earlier.

PART 2

Business

CHAPTER 5

Jumping Ship

By mid-2004, I had come to the conclusion that I was ready to make a move from Fidelity. I had saved money, my children were grown (at least physically), and I felt ready in terms of my skills. Now I needed to evaluate the other risks associated with starting a new venture.

I had to answer several critical questions about forming a company. Could I do this on my own or did I need a business partner? What exact services would we provide? And who would be the brave individuals who would pay us to manage their money? After I had those questions in mind, the process began to fall into place like a puzzle. I also recognized that once the vision took form, I needed to clear-mindedly compare it with what I now had: a great career at a wonderful company with fantastic compensation. The prospect of undertaking this analysis was scary yet also intoxicating.

Every step demanded that I recognize the full dimensions of the particular jigsaw piece, each with its risks and its rewards, before moving on to the next. Of course, each question branched into additional inquiries, and it was important that I focus my attention on the tenets of practical risk-taking as a means of evaluating my options.

SOLO FLIGHT OR NOT?

The first question—whether I should start the business on my own—was relatively easy to answer. Although I was a fund manager at a major, nationally known institution, I did not have a list of extremely wealthy clients—as someone at Goldman Sachs Asset Management might have—who could move with me to my new address. I also realized that my gender might work against me. Perhaps I was imagining that liability, but I believed that most decisions about hiring an investment professional were made by men, and I wasn't confident that a critical mass of rich men would flock to Karen Firestone's new asset management company unless I had a male cofounder who was well known in the business.

I called a few close friends in the investment field and discreetly asked whether they knew of any senior investment professionals who might consider leaving their companies to create a start-up. I talked quietly to many people in Boston, but only one lead clicked. I had met David Scudder, a former partner at Wellington Management, many years earlier during my summer internship there. Because Wellington has a tightly enforced policy that encourages all partners to retire at age sixty, David, who was older than I, had left six years before to work at Harvard Management, the entity that oversees the vast Harvard University endowment. When we met, the period of his Wellington noncompete clause had expired and he was free to cofound a new investment company.

While at Harvard Management, David succeeded in completing a creative and groundbreaking accomplishment in nonprofit history. The endowment had a fabulous investment record, and David, with the aid of Harvard's attorneys, discovered an ingenious means of allowing donors to co-invest a trust with the university by committing to donate to Harvard either a fixed amount annually or a remainder after a given number of years. A legal judgment supported the practice, and Harvard experienced a massive influx of new gifts.

OPPOSITES ATTRACT

David and I liked each other and we had many acquaintances in common, but our backgrounds and networks were different. He was a well-loved, statesmanlike, traditional presence with deep roots at Harvard, board seats on many local charitable institutions, membership at many mainstream institutions, and a desire, as did I, to start something new.

In contrast, I was a poor Jewish kid from Brighton, a working-class section of Boston dominated, when I was young, by the presence of the Catholic Church, which had massive land holdings including the cardinal's residence. I catapulted myself out of Brighton, suppressed my Boston accent, went to Harvard College and Harvard Business School, and married a smart, funny, and kind Harvard graduate from a well-established family in Boston. Despite my educational credentials and my husband's background, I was still a career woman from Brighton without a "book" of business, and I had spent almost half my life at Fidelity.

One of the biggest risks to a start-up is that the founders will run out of cash. David and I both had capital and could forgo a salary for the first couple of years if necessary. He had family members who would likely hire us as well as strong relationships from several trusteeships. Between these accounts and our combined assets from his days at Wellington and mine at Fidelity, we would be in reasonably good shape to launch our company.

The strength of the relationship between partners in a new venture often determines the success or failure of the company. In my case, I needed to consider how likely it would be that David would get cold feet and back out. After several conversations, David seemed both very enthusiastic and extremely committed.

Was he being honest about his own financial strength? My friends at Wellington confirmed that David was well off. How was his health? Although he was nearly two decades older than I, David's health was incredible. There are few people at a height of six-foot-three with as low a weight-per-inch quotient, and anyone who can keep up with David's stride on his long, twice-daily walks to and from his train deserves a gold medal.

Budding entrepreneurs have to weigh the need, the desire, and the availability of an appropriate partner with the risk of eventual dissent over money and direction. David and I would each own equal shares of our new company, and jointly we would hold two-thirds ownership of the firm, with the younger partners owning the balance. We were not willing to risk losing control to a group of minority shareholders, even if they were talented junior partners. We had the financial ability to retain control, so we did.

Through the years, David and I have never had a major disagreement, and when he told me that he was thinking of selling his shares in anticipation of retirement, we agreed to a deal in which I purchased enough shares to gain a majority interest. I have observed many partnerships disintegrate through battles over hiring, compensation, new-product introduction, and allocation of resources. Luckily, unlike technology or biotech companies, which require substantial capital and generally must rely on venture capital or angel investors, we could fund the start-up ourselves for the first couple of years until we broke even.

We each agreed at the beginning to contribute $1 million, obviously not a trivial amount, but the company would hopefully one day reimburse us if and when we became profitable. We were hardly building this start-up on a shoestring, but we felt certain that we would not need to invest additional funds. We also knew that if we ended up losing our contributions, we would not need to change our lifestyle—a critical consideration when right sizing a new venture.

RIGHT OFFERINGS

The next big question was how to define exactly what we would offer as our services and how we might set ourselves apart from a field of highly competent competitors. We wanted to manage or oversee as high a percentage of the financial assets of our clients as possible. Neither of us was interested in starting a hedge fund—a crowded asset class, and one in which it is very difficult to succeed.

I like to say that if you hold up both hands with fingers outstretched, you indicate more than the number of people in the world who are capable of managing a hedge fund well for more than fifteen years. Although I had personally shorted stocks years before, my experience was limited solely to the biotechnology industry, over a relatively short period of time. Neither David nor I had ever managed a hedge fund, and we both wanted to concentrate on areas in which we had extensive knowledge and experience.

We both envisioned offering a range of investment options more expansive than stock or bond portfolios, somewhat comparable to what endowments provide for their institutions. David coined the term "contemporary endowment model," which conjures an image of highly liquid assets, such as stocks and some bonds as well as hedge funds, and less liquid investments, including real estate, venture capital, and private equity. What we could manage internally would depend on the backgrounds of our staff, starting with U.S.-based stock portfolios, which was my expertise and the area I would direct.

By offering investments across a broad range of assets, we would strategically distribute the risk by not having all of our performance focused on one strategy, a concept I learned at Fidelity with the industry-specific sector funds, one of which would always top the charts for any time period. We intended to choose outside managers for most non-U.S. equity allocations, since most of our investment experience was domestic. We would also focus more on taxes and liquidity needs than a traditional endowment model.

With my concept and a solid partner in place, the next obvious and critical question on my list was: Who would make up our clientele? The potential risk was that we would open for business and no one would walk in the door. All good ideas need buyers or they merely fade away.

Between our two families and a few trusting friends, we thought that we would have about $100 million in assets under management when we started, the fees on which, at 1 percent, would cover our expenses if David and I did not take any salary. We projected that we could double our assets over the first two years, after which we would break even, including a salary for ourselves. Of course, if the market turned south, we lost money for our clients, or we failed to pick up any new clients, we both knew we were doomed. I imagined that I could crawl back to Fidelity with my tail between my legs and beg, and David would retire. However, neither of us believed we would fail.

PERSONAL RISK

What personal risk factors did I need to address as I prepared to start my business? I recognized three distinctive categories: financial well-being, long-term security, and reputation. The relative importance of these factors varies from person to person—age, family situation, and current net worth are all critical individual considerations. The tenets of risk-taking apply to all three categories in varying proportions.

The compensation risk was obvious: I would be making much less money (in fact, no money) for at least a couple of years. It was entirely possible that my annual compensation would never again be as high as it had been at Fidelity. I played that line over and over again in my head until it sank in. My dream about starting a business and creating a new platform for myself was not about making a killing financially. I was comfortable with the fact that I had previously made a lot of money but would now potentially make far less for many years to come. However, I was unwilling to risk so much that my lifestyle would suffer.

The first time I was given the chance to buy Fidelity stock was in 1985. At nearly every annual review I was offered even more stock and always agreed to the terms, even though the capital outlays could be very high. To say no was to never be asked again.

As the mutual fund industry grew and Fidelity became the dominant player, thanks to our excellent fund results, marketing strength, and customer service, the institution's worth grew exponentially, as did all the shareholders' stock value. Anyone who left Fidelity was obliged to sell her stock back to the company.

Because the shareholders knew the price per share, I could calculate my stake, and it was substantial. Besides the generous shares I had accumulated over my tenure, I had also saved money from my salary and invested in the stock market. My husband continued to work in his family's business. Unless we decided to buy a Gulfstream, travel incessantly to five-star hotels around the world, produce films, or donate a new building to the nonprofit of my choice, the failure of my new business would not affect our lifestyle. I have often said that I give thanks to Mr. Johnson every day for bringing me into his company, not that he either interviewed me or made the job offer, but he set the tone and the style at his company, which brought me into its core.

When contemplating leaving an established company to found a start-up, it's critical that you analyze carefully your ability to cover the new business expenses and to survive a period of limited income. Many entrepreneurs resist confronting what would truly happen to their daily existence if the gallery, restaurant, real estate development, or hedge fund they were creating never got off the ground. While I would hate failing, I knew that I could weather the storm financially. I wanted to make money; our start-up was no act of altruism, and I thought we had a business strategy and structure that would be solidly profitable in the coming years.

As I considered my move, it was clear that there would be major consequences of leaving such a respected financial institution and the job security it had provided for most of my adult life. Of course, I could have been overstating how safe my job was, but as a twenty-two-year veteran, I assumed that my skills and my contributions were well known.

Job security was among the least of my concerns, however. More worrisome was the possibility that the intensity of my current position might lead to burnout. I considered my greatest risk the potential harm to my reputation. I had built my reputation over a two-decade career, both inside and outside Fidelity, as someone who worked hard, understood how to analyze and pick stocks, and did so with professionalism. Over the course of my career, I had developed hundreds of relationships and acquaintances in the business, building a network that had great personal value.

While people might have initially been surprised about my impending departure from Fidelity, and perhaps may even have thought I was foolish, I wanted them to be rooting for me. I would be lying if I didn't admit that I also wanted to score a victory for women entrepreneurs, particularly those few of us in finance. In addition, this was my opportunity to establish my own brand, independent of Fidelity, and I was aware that a desire for independence was one of the key drivers in my decision.

I felt confident that I had applied the tenets of sensible risk-taking to the formative stages of my new enterprise. David was a partner who made sense for me. We had the appropriate capital with which to bankroll the project at a size that was right for our start-up. The timing was right for me and for him. We had both spent our careers building the skills we needed to run this new firm, and I felt comfortable with my organizational strengths. Finally, we both understood that this venture would not be easy, that every projection we made was only that—a column of numbers on paper that could be far from accurate. We had our eyes wide open, but we both wanted to keep the momentum going and take the plunge.

I told David that I had come to my decision. Upon reflection and consideration of my future ambitions, both professionally and personally, I decided the time had come to leave Fidelity. I thought we should begin looking for office space immediately, assemble our team, and choose the date on which we would deliver our resignations. Just saying the word "resignation" gave me chills, but it wasn't a fearful chill, as I now embraced the risk that had kept me up at night struggling with the decision.

LEGAL LIGHTNING

Deciding to leave a company and a job to which I had devoted so much of my life was just the beginning of the work that I needed to do to lay a firm groundwork for our new venture. Nearly every day for months on end David and I made decisions that were critical—and laden with risk.

One of our earliest challenges arose months before the SEC even granted us approval to trade accounts. We had hired an eminent Boston law firm to service our new company. All investment firms must create a series of documents, including a compliance manual that outlines crucial corporate procedures and practices for the firm. This manual might detail services offered, policies on trading, data security systems, privacy policies, investment guidelines, and the employee code of ethics. We asked our attorney to draft our compliance manual.

A few weeks later, the firm sent us a draft. Based on the various fonts and line spacing, the document seemed to be a reassembly of a few previously completed compliance manuals. David and I knew that there would be several other iterations of this manual, which was only the first of the several major filings that we would need to provide to the SEC before it authorized us as a Registered Investment Advisor. The bill for that first draft appeared soon after: an eye-popping $22,000.

Between hyperventilating breaths, I contacted our attorney. All I could visualize were six-figure legal bills, which we could barely afford. We would be out of business before we even opened. One risk we had never envisioned was being strapped for cash before we started conducting business. When our lawyer called me back, I explained that we were shocked and troubled by the cost. While I am sure that large organizations and even individuals expect their legal bills to mount in parabolic fashion, my partner and I were woefully naive.

To reduce the scale of this risk—to right size it—I opted for a solution that I explained to our lawyer. I would write the compliance manual myself, which would not violate any regulation. When completed, I would show the attorneys my version, which they could edit but not bill for, because we were at our limit for the preliminary documents. Friends' warnings of the perils of starting a company played over and over in my head. Our attorney grudgingly agreed, and I immediately began contacting friends in the business, begging them to share their compliance manuals and code of ethics documents with me. After some intense cramming on regulatory and financial terminology, I pulled together a document that the firm's associate considered passable, canvassed those same friends for the name of a smaller law firm that better suited our needs and our checkbook, and relieved our former attorney of further duties.

As we prepared to launch our new company, which we called Aureus Asset Management, I realized that we had taken on an outsized risk through something as innocuous as legal counsel; collapse was merely one budget-breaking bill away. Luckily, however, we solved the problem through the use of our own skills and common sense.

The decision to leave a comfortable job and launch a new venture must include evaluating the risks of any alternative path—financial risks, together with reputational and psychological risks. Once we make a commitment to one direction, we need to create a rigorous plan that incorporates the financial and nonfinancial elements of the new enterprise, as well as the options available when progress deviates from the original blueprint, which it almost always will. Entrepreneurs, in particular, need to be prepared to sacrifice salary, time, and comfort—considering all the risks carefully ahead of time will help reduce the possibility of unpleasant surprises.

CHAPTER 6

Building a Business

Creating a business entails multiple risks and hurdles, some of which you can anticipate but many of which are surprising. Ten years into our venture, I am rarely startled when business is not "usual"; instead, I concentrate on how to appreciate and learn from each new episode, even if my natural inclination is to scream in frustration. That is where addressing risk sensibly comes in handy.

There are no handbooks that outline the risks and hurdles of each unique start-up or established enterprise. Challenges arise over time and require continuous reassessment. The following are illustrations of enterprises in transition and the executives in charge who faced critical tests.

TRANSFORMATION

The formidable stumbling blocks my partner and I faced in our early years are nothing new to Jeff Flowers and David Friend, two serial entrepreneurs who have created five technology companies together. I spoke with them about one of those companies—Carbonite—at the headquarters of Storiant, their latest start-up.

As computer engineers, they were intrigued with the idea that individuals rarely backed up the important data located on their home computers or personal devices. Jeff's wife and David's daughter lost all their photos when their hard drives crashed, propelling Jeff to design a novel software backup system. His creation would later yield Carbonite, a company that delivers "all-you-can-eat" backup storage to consumers for an extremely low price.

Jeff, amiable and effusive, with a Georgian drawl and dressed in the programmer's uniform of jeans and a casual shirt, explained that individual consumers, unlike businesses, were motivated more by cheap and slow than by fast but expensive. David, the contemplative partner, who arrived at Storiant's headquarters via a jog from his townhouse in Boston's Back Bay, agreed that the storage of individual files such as photo albums is not particularly time sensitive.

A market research study showed that 92 percent of people did not store their personal computer data anywhere other than on their own device and did not purchase external storage because the process was thought to be complicated and expensive. With this realization, a start-up was born. According to David, Jeff figured out a "brilliant new database architecture that was targeted to do backups slower and a lot cheaper than the standard procedure offered by legacy databases."

They recognized certain risks. Would one of the major storage players, such as EMC, move into this market aggressively with a low-cost product, even if it meant cannibalizing their much pricier offerings? The founders knew they had a strong product at a great price, but they also knew the unpredictability of consumer tastes and the importance of hitting a trend at just the right time. According to Jeff, "The waves keep coming, but you need to be on your board at the exact moment when the big one rolls into shore, or you miss out on your chance."

For these reasons, Jeff and David kept their options open. They were experts at what they did and relied on their skills to create a fantastic storage solution. However, they could not be sure whether they were right timing the introduction of direct-to-consumer storage sales, so they decided to sell through dual channels. They partnered with other companies in the field and also marketed directly to consumers. They stressed that building flexibility into the organizational strategy mitigates the risk of being stuck with an approach that might quickly be overtaken by a competitor or unpopular with customers.

In hindsight, I realize that we were very lucky at Aureus to manage our clients' assets across different formats such as direct investing in stocks and allocations to external managers like hedge funds. Initially, we considered the rationale for this broad allocation to be the implementation of a diversification strategy, until we saw that it saved us from excessive risk exposure to one asset class that might be underperforming at the time.

Right timing is the difference between a terrific, career-defining stock selection and an unmemorable dud. A good idea only deserves the adjective if the timing is right for it to work. The space between "on the verge" and "maybe in two years" is as wide as the spread between first and tenth place in the Kentucky Derby.

Carbonite's first critical test on market tastes and timing came in 2011. The company had, in fact, caught the wave of consumer demand for data storage at low prices. Founded in 2009, Carbonite had grown to a $36 million business by 2011. As good as that sounds, Jeff and David recognized that they might need to change the direction of the company in order to better serve the portion of the market that was really growing. Although they were marketing and advertising to consumers, a growing segment of their customer base included small businesses whose needs were broader than those of most individuals.

The founders wanted to ensure a right-sized risk by focusing more attention on small businesses, where they could sell bundled subscriptions with higher average selling prices, better retention rates, and lower support costs. Many on the management team thought this strategy was a mistake because they did not believe the small corporate market presented enough opportunity.

Jeff and David were adamant that small businesses needed backup that would ensure they could quickly resume operations following any disaster scenario, and these small companies would gravitate toward such a system if it were offered at a fraction of the price of other systems. Carbonite already had a fantastic product that would apply perfectly to a commercial clientele. However, the founders met resistance within their organization. More than half of the management staff dug in their heels in opposition, insisting that Carbonite was a consumer business and that consumers should remain the priority.

David, who was CEO, insisted on broadening Carbonite's market. Those who resisted the firm's small business initiative either left or were asked to leave. Jeff and David felt that everyone in management should be on board with the overall strategy. They were so committed to this strategy that the company acquired a firm that offered the missing pieces of technology they needed in this market plus an existing client list.

Over the following nine months, David and Jeff worried that they had sabotaged Carbonite, dooming it to failure. It was too late to turn back. Yet, gradually, sales to small businesses gained momentum, proving the merits of the shift in direction. This channel today represents half of the firm's sales, $123 million in 2014, and continues to grow much faster than the once-coveted consumer storage business.

Carbonite's leaders had correctly identified the huge risk to their enterprise if they did not enter the small business market and the large opportunity available to them if they acted immediately. They were appropriately skeptical of members of their team who insisted that they remain in their current market. If David and Jeff had not had insight into the impending threat and the boldness to take the company in a radically different direction, Carbonite might not exist today.

FASHION FORWARDING

When business is booming we may forget to notice that the landscape around us is changing, sometimes very rapidly, and that risks are building. Sara Campbell is a talented entrepreneur who ran a successful company for almost two decades, until her two biggest customers botched their own expansion strategies, leaving Sara dangling on the brink of financial ruin.

Unlike some fashion designers who wear all black or sport outlandish signature accessories to go with their year-round tans, Sara Campbell could be an advertising executive or even a college professor. She has crystal-clear blue eyes, a dazzling smile, and dark, chin-length hair accented with grey, and she wears colorful, well-tailored dresses that are preppy chic with a hip twist. Sara grew up loving to sew, and by the time she was in ninth grade she had become accomplished enough to teach sewing to neighborhood women and their children. She was good with numbers, unlike many artists, and knew, when she received her master's degree from Massachusetts College of Art, that she would ultimately work for herself.

Sara first went to work for Sister Corita Kent, the well-known artist whom Sara credits as her mentor and inspiration. Sister Corita—a nun who left her convent in California, but not her order, to move East—used her pop art as a medium to protest the Vietnam War and promote the countercultural message of peace and love. Her most enduring monument adorns the Boston gas tank, visible from one of the most frequented highways in the city, with bright splashes of color that include an image resembling Ho Chi Minh's profile. Sara worked in Corita's gallery and then became a partner, designing textiles herself and eventually producing limited editions of her own clothing designs.

In 1985, Sara set out on her own for the first time. She incorporated, moved to a storefront in Boston's South End, a marginal neighborhood on the brink of gentrification, and began designing and manufacturing her clothing line, called Sara Campbell. Her clothes are for women who dress up for work or simply to lunch; she describes her style as having classic, body-conforming shapes with a bit of "whimsy and a splash of color."

Because no bank would lend her a dime, Sara borrowed $25,000 from her mother. She was young, skilled, not yet married, could invest countless hours, and was confident that she had chosen the right time for her new venture. She partnered with Peter Wheeler, design director at Finnish fabric and design company Marimekko, and they embarked on a long, close, and productive partnership.

For years the company's sales were almost entirely wholesale, and it designed and manufactured a limited number of styles for third parties including Talbots, Nordstrom, and Laura Ashley. In 1992, the company was earning nearly $1 million in profit, which grew steadily for the next decade. Although the margins on wholesale trade pale compared with those in retail, Sara's private-label business generated more than $20 million in sales by the early years of the millennium.

After nearly a decade of growth, however, the entire landscape for Sara Campbell suddenly began shifting. In 2008, the financial world collapsed, along with Sara's biggest customers. Talbots, her largest client at the time, was crumbling under the weight of overexpansion and poor management. Laura Ashley was disintegrating in similar fashion, a victim of the recession and the resulting decline in consumer spending, coupled with a steady rise of increasingly hip competitors such as J.Crew, H&M, and Zara. Suddenly, orders began to evaporate. Sara's outsized dependence on two customers, both of which were in distress, had created a considerable risk that she was now confronting. Not only were her revenues collapsing but her company still had production commitments and excess capacity in every aspect of her enterprise.

Sara and Peter knew that they had to reinvent themselves. Perhaps they might have anticipated that their largest customers were failing in a cutthroat retail environment increasingly dominated by brands that could aggressively drive major new trends. Both Talbots and Laura Ashley ignored signs that their loyal consumers were abandoning their merchandise. Sara considered how she could even the odds.

Salvation appeared at first in the form of an accomplished investor who began courting Sara with an eye toward turning the Sara Campbell line into the next hot retail brand. The overture came at a time when Sara desperately needed cash to stay afloat, and over a period of several months, Sara Campbell LTD received an infusion of new capital.

According to Sara, the relationship with her new partner was troubled from the start. Sara and Peter had been calling their own shots for many years, and their investor was demanding. Disagreement over the terms of the agreement and the roles of the parties threatened a tangle of litigation, and Sara and Peter ended the partnership with their investor. Fortunately, the cash they had received initially allowed them to survive in the short term, but they needed to scramble to pay that money back and keep the business running.

Sara admits that she was naive and hadn't listened closely enough to her attorney, who advised her to be very careful in her dealings with investors. Sara had not listened because she needed the money fast, but in her haste she disregarded the tenet of relying on knowledge and experience, in this case her attentive attorney.

Sara's company was struggling financially, and filing for bankruptcy was an option, but she and Peter resisted and were determined to stay solvent. They instead borrowed what they could from family and friends, a strategy that might have saved them a lot of headaches if they had pursued that course from the outset.

They were still committed to production runs at several factories but no longer had orders from their former major customers, so Sara and Peter made the audacious choice to expand to several new Sara Campbell retail shops that would carry only the designer's product. It was a desperate move, and it worked.

The recession helped Peter find attractively priced retail space in several locations along the East Coast. The company faced down the risk of bankruptcy, and not only survived but thrived in its new locations. After years of recession fatigue, women began to spend more on apparel and Sara sought to catch that wave. She and Peter have opened an additional twelve Sara Campbell boutiques along the East Coast, from Massachusetts to Florida, and the stores are now producing $8 million in annual merchandise sales at a healthy profit margin.

Sara Campbell LTD no longer has an outsized risk associated with two dominant customers. However, the founders must now be careful about trusting projections for their many retail stores. In each location, there are unique revenue and cost variables such as weather, regional economic strength, rent escalation, and sales staff pay. Sara and Peter need to be realistic and commit to appropriate inventory levels while taking into consideration the many variables that can lead to a positive (or negative) retail season.

When examining forecasts, Sara and Peter recognize the tradeoff between risks connected to the financial strength of a couple of customers and risks associated with their own initiatives and projections; they vastly prefer the latter. Sara Campbell is growing as a brand with a loyal following that reflects the company's connection with today's retail culture.

After surviving a perfect storm of negative events, accentuated by extreme exposure to the fate of two private-label customers, Sara right sized her positioning in the women's apparel sector by building on her strengths as a designer and operator. She rejected the suggestion to file for bankruptcy because she trusted her skills and raised enough money to implement her strategy. It worked.

Sara hopes that she can eventually sell Sara Campbell LTD to a larger retailer or, perhaps, to a private equity firm, several of which have purchased apparel brands with expansion potential in the past decade. After persevering through several years of business nightmares, she felt she deserved to carry her namesake enterprise to its just reward.

SAVING LIVES

Henri Termeer is one of the architects of the biotechnology industry. No one would dispute that he—along with Walter Gilbert, Phil Sharp, Gabe Schmergel, George Rathmann, Herb Boyer, and Bob Swanson— is among the pioneers of the field that has grown from an emerging industry in 1976 to a sector that generated sales of more than $100 billion in 2015.

Henri and I spoke about his start in the Netherlands, where he was born and educated, and the significant risks he encountered on his journey to becoming chief executive of Genzyme, the third-largest biotech company in the world. Henri built valuable but scattered assets and intellectual property into a global corporation that developed lifesaving drugs, produced annual revenues in the billions, and ultimately sold for more than $20 billion.

After earning his MBA, Henri took a job in 1973 at Baxter Travenol, the Chicago-based leader in plasma and blood replacement products. He was sent to Europe, where he quickly moved up the ranks to become general manager in Germany, working under Gabe Schmergel, who ran the European division. Having proven himself overseas, Henri was summoned back to the United States, where, in 1979, he became vice president of Baxter's biotechnology division, located in Los Angeles. At the time, the biotech industry was in its infancy—the first firms emerged in the mid-1970s, and included Biogen and Genetics Institute, founded by Gabe Schmergel, Henri's boss when they worked for Baxter in Germany.

Biotechnology is a term that describes the use of living organisms, including bacteria and other living cells, as the production mechanism for drugs composed of biological matter rather than of chemical compounds, the traditional raw material for therapeutics. The industry was rooted in the growing scientific understanding of how DNA and genes impact disease. Henri saw biotech as the new frontier, and he wanted to be not only a player but a groundbreaker.

In the early 1980s, venture capitalists were circling Baxter, raiding the company for talent to run the latest start-ups. They called Henri in August 1983 and he flew to Boston to meet a group of eight scientists who worked for a small firm called Genzyme, a play on *genetics* and *enzyme*. He had never heard of the company before, but there was no reason he should have. Genzyme was located on Kneeland Street in downtown Boston, halfway between Chinatown and a district known as the Combat Zone, which was chock-full of seedy bars and strip clubs, and reeked of alcohol.

Henri met with several MIT scientists who were considering joining the advisory board on Genzyme. They discussed the potential for a novel drug being developed by one of the founders of the company, Dr. Henry Blair, to treat a rare genetic disorder called Gaucher disease, a condition caused by an enzyme deficiency that causes multiple physical and developmental challenges, and which often leads to early death. Blair's intent was to harvest enzymes from placentas and inject them into patients, which would, hopefully, reverse the symptoms.

Henri weighed the risk of leaving a lucrative job at Baxter for a venture-backed start-up. He was attracted to the idea of helping very sick children. Also, Genzyme was in Boston, halfway between Los Angeles and Europe, where his family lived, including his ex-wife, who had moved to London with their son. Additionally, Genzyme had one of the industry's greatest assets, a shipping department, confirming that it actually had sales, unlike most start-up biotech firms.

Henri visited Gabe Schmergel, his former boss and mentor at Baxter, who was now the CEO of a start-up biotechnology company called Genetics Institute. Henri found Schmergel toiling away in a dreary space in the bowels of the Brigham and Women's Hospital in Boston. Gingerly, Henri asked his friend, who looked disheveled and frustrated, whether he enjoyed his work. With a gleam in his eyes, Schmergel said, "It's so hard. But I love every minute of it." Henri was single, ambitious, determined, and ready to leave Baxter. There was little downside. Henri placed the call; he would take the job as CEO of Genzyme Corporation.

Knowing that the chance of success with any one drug is low, Henri was intent on developing several opportunities at once. This way, he could right size the exposure of Genzyme to any one program. He hedged his bets beyond the Gaucher product into other enzyme programs. Genzyme went public in 1986, raising $25 million—a paltry sum by today's standards. The next three years were very active, highlighted by an acquisition of Integrated Genetics, which offered mammalian cell production technology that Genzyme needed, a move to a new headquarters in the developing Kendall Square neighborhood of Cambridge, and most importantly, a filing for approval with the FDA for Ceredase, the brand name given to the Gaucher disease drug.

At the 1990 FDA Advisory Panel meeting for Ceredase, Henri realized that the specter of the HIV epidemic hung over the proceedings. Despite the clinical benefit demonstrated by Ceredase, there was a risk that the drug would fail to get the necessary votes of the Advisory Panel because of fear surrounding the possibility of HIV infection from human tissue.

Henri felt that he could ease the panel members' insecurity and improve the chance of a positive vote for approval by testifying himself. He had spent a decade at Baxter, the world's leading plasma and blood products company, and knew his material cold. Yet, Henri still faced the risk of failing to win approval for Ceredase, even with his knowledge and experience. In a highly unusual and intensely debated move within the Genzyme group assembled in Bethesda, Henri took a seat at the microphone.

The scale of risk to Genzyme was enormous, the timing was critical, and Henri knew the data as well as anyone. The tactic of the CEO speaking directly to the committee worked, as the panel members recommended that the FDA approve Ceredase.

Through the 1990s, sales for Ceredase, one of the most expensive drugs in the world, at $350,000 per patient, grew exponentially. Despite attacks on the pricing, Henri never wavered, maintaining that price parity across geographies assured that Genzyme could provide free drugs where reimbursement was unavailable. He has been a champion for transparency about cost, uniform pricing, and accessibility to the poor and uninsured for decades.

STRUGGLE

When, in the early 1990s, Henri Termeer and his management announced plans to break ground for a new manufacturing plant in North Carolina, Bill Weld, the governor of Massachusetts, asked him to reconsider that decision. In an effort to reinvigorate the state's manufacturing sector, Weld suggested that Genzyme build the plant in a prominent location in Boston, along the Charles River, visible to twenty million drivers per year. Henri right sized the financial risk by requesting and receiving many favorable conditions from the Commonwealth. Weld met his requests, and the Allston plant has been a successful landmark of the biotechnology industry for years.

Genzyme's most dramatic challenge arose out of a bounty of riches. As Henri explains, it is impossible to develop drugs sequentially, with each product smoothly and predictably following the last. In 2006, the FDA and every European governing body approved Myozyme for Pompe disease, another enzyme-deficit disorder affecting a small population, for which the diagnosis was generally fatal. Remarkably, of the babies studied in the small Phase 3 clinical trial, all the treated infants survived but 98 percent of the control group died within a year.

Genzyme found itself unprepared for the onslaught of demand. Obviously, every family with a child afflicted by Pompe wanted the drug, and quickly. Elected officials in the United States and Europe were pleading on behalf of constituents, some of whom had chained themselves to the gates of the Spanish Ministry of Health. Genzyme, surprised by the resounding conclusiveness of the study and the speed of global approvals, had very limited supply and an inadequate capacity to meet the sudden demand for Myozyme.

Genzyme had postponed the construction of a new manufacturing plant in Framingham, Massachusetts, until it was confident that the drug worked. The board and management believed that beginning construction on a new facility for Myozyme before the results were conclusive could be a costly mistake. Considering that the total construction and regulatory costs of a new drug production facility are over $300 million, it is not surprising that executives and their boards favor moving cautiously.

They bet wrong. Genzyme was caught flat-footed, with no ability to treat the hundreds of children Myozyme would benefit. As Henri said, when the head of the European Common Market called repeatedly, accusing Genzyme of ignoring dying patients, he couldn't keep saying, "We'll get you the drug in two years."

At an emergency board meeting, the company decided to authorize two new reactors for the recently approved drugs at the Allston facility, which had previously only manufactured the drug for Gaucher disease. They were now scrambling through a process that required methodical attention to thousands of details. In hindsight, it's clear that Genzyme violated the tenet of relying on knowledge, skill, and experience, and it did so in an area that is exceedingly delicate and complex: a biotechnology manufacturing facility. Employees needed to vacate offices and move into the corridors, which were jammed with desks, chairs, and boxes. The plant oozed urgency and unconditional commitment to fulfilling the needs of patients.

FDA inspectors arrived in mid-2009. While Henri was at his home in Maine, he got the call every biopharmaceutical executive fears. A virus was killing the Chinese hamster ovary (CHO) cells commonly used as hosts for biotechnology products. It was a black swan event that no one in the company had ever envisioned.[1] They needed to close the factory immediately. Seventy vendors took part in dismantling, analyzing, and reconstructing every aspect of the Allston plant over the next three to four months. The company's stock sank more than 40 percent, and the press railed about the plant's failings.

Henri describes this as the most agonizing period of his life. He traveled around the world, meeting with patients and their families to reassure them that Genzyme would be manufacturing the drugs again soon, and that new operations in Belgium and Framingham would open shortly.

He now admits that the risks of not building the new plant were greater than the risk of building the factory two years earlier than it was needed. Though the final clinical results for Myozyme were unknown in 2006, the early signs of efficacy strongly suggested that the drug would ultimately work. Building in redundancy would have avoided the plant shutdown and the damages that ensued.

When stocks drop sharply after extraordinary events, corporate raiders begin to circle. First Carl Icahn initiated a proxy attack on Genzyme in its weakened state, which Henri successfully averted by accepting Icahn's demands for two board seats. By 2010, the new factories were fully operational and Allston had reopened. Henri was relieved, yet his feelings turned out to be premature.

Chris Viehbacher, CEO of the large French drug company Sanofi, called out of the blue to offer his "help" in avoiding an unfriendly takeover, but Henri politely spurned his advances. Genzyme was in recovery mode; it just needed time to regain its stride.

But Henri didn't have time. Genzyme stock had fallen by 40 percent, from more than $80 in August 2008 to the high $40s. Once a public company becomes vulnerable, particularly when buyers' stock prices are high and borrowing costs are low, there is little defense against losing independence other than making a large acquisition yourself.

Henri looked but did not find an appropriate firm to buy. Sanofi came back to him with a buyout offer that Genzyme's board refused. Henri had spent nearly thirty years building Genzyme into an industry leader with normalized earnings exceeding $400 million on over $4 billion in sales from multiple products, with many more to come. He wanted to remain independent. However, Viehbacher and the Sanofi board were determined, continuing to raise their offer. Finally, in April of 2011, Genzyme agreed to the terms of the takeover at $74 per share, or a total of $20 billion.

The Genzyme division of Sanofi is thriving and is a foothold for Sanofi in the exciting world of biotechnology. However, the outcome for Henri Termeer was bittersweet. Although he walked away a very rich man, he feels certain that Genzyme's stock price would have appreciated two or three times the purchase price, at least matching the overall biotechnology sector.

Genzyme's situation illustrates the use and misuse of the tenets of risk-taking. The company waited too long to start construction on another plant, neglecting to right time this facility, but then proceeded to rush production of the new product before the manufacturing complexities were well understood and processes totally locked down. Genzyme paid for these oversights with the loss of its independence.

Henri Termeer continues as a founder and active investor in many start-up health-care companies and serves on several large corporate and nonprofit boards. However, he will always wonder if the outcome for Genzyme would have been different had he planned better and trusted that the scientific research effort, which he had nurtured for decades, would work as he expected it should.

The risks associated with each of these examples, from Carbonite to Sara Campbell to Genzyme, highlight the challenges that businesses and their leaders encounter as the companies grow and environments change. Carbonite needed to accept the risk of targeting new markets. Sara Campbell's core market disappeared almost entirely, and the company was forced to the brink of bankruptcy but emerged stronger after the founder leveraged her strengths as a designer and a retailer. The case of Henri Termeer and Genzyme incorporates elements of right sizing, right timing, relying on knowledge and experience, and maintaining healthy skepticism, demonstrated from start-up stage right through the eventual sale of the company.

CHAPTER 7

Surviving Crisis

The outcome of a business challenge can range from highly profitable and effective to disturbing and costly. An ad agency in the running to create a new marketing campaign for a consumer products company might lose the competition but develop a catchy concept that can be reworked successfully for another client. Winning the bid for a large construction project may yield a huge contract and significant prestige, but what good is it if the job's cost overruns erode all profit? We can apply the four tenets of sensible risk-taking even when risks are unclear and despite possibly tenuous outcomes.

CRASH CONNECTION

I have lived through several gut-wrenching periods during my investment career, waking each morning with a sick feeling in my stomach. My anxiety stemmed from a sense of helplessness that I had no great ideas to offset the losses in my fund or in the accounts I was managing, which were owned by people who trusted me with their hard-earned dollars. My Fidelity colleagues and I referred to this as the "imposter complex"—you feel like you have absolutely no qualifications, and are simply posing as a mutual fund manager. While bull markets are confidence-producing events, bear markets deplete the confidence of almost every investment professional I know.

The global crash of 2008, ignited by the collapse of the subprime mortgage market and implosion of Bear Stearns and Lehman Brothers, was the scariest market atmosphere I have ever experienced. I hope that it will continue to hold that distinction for the rest of my life. On October 12, 2007, the S&P 500 peaked at 1,561 after being on a sharp uptrend for several years, and then proceeded to plummet over the next seventeen months, along with almost every financial market in the world.

The crash destroyed innumerable businesses in the financial industry, as well as in many others. At my firm, Aureus Asset Management, I experienced the debacle of 2007–2008 as both an investor and a recent entrepreneur. Most firms like mine bill clients based on a percentage of assets under management, so when the market tanks, assets collapse—and so do fees. While we had been reducing stocks as a percentage of our portfolios, it was not enough to avoid the carnage. Our clients were losing money, our company's revenues were eroding, and our costs were not dropping in the slightest. I was reluctant to power my computer on every morning at the office.

The market that had generated vast wealth over the previous decade was now rapidly pulverizing those very fortunes. Two such victims were Erin and Nick Dempsey,* married tech entrepreneurs from Silicon Valley. The two had met at Notre Dame in the early 1990s, when both spent excessive time at the computer lab writing code and playing video games.

The Dempseys moved their home base to the Bay Area, where

---

*Erin and Nick Dempsey are composites.

Erin continued her graduate studies in computer engineering and Nick started a small software consulting business. The large Silicon Valley technology companies were increasingly worried about secrets leaking to competitors both domestic and foreign. A number of these tech firms hired Nick as a consultant, and he eventually used the skills he learned on these projects to found his own security software business. Erin joined him at the company, which grew at an astonishing speed.

Over the next decade, the Dempseys had two children and their enterprise continued to expand, despite the fact that the competitive landscape became fierce. Erin and Nick received an unsolicited offer from a multinational corporation intent on expanding its cybersecurity division, and they sold their company for $100 million in cash.

Nick had grown up in New Jersey with his stockbroker dad commuting each day to Wall Street. After the tech bubble burst in 2000, his father, a longtime employee of a major brokerage firm, lost his job and never returned to financial services. The entire family became suspicious of financial institutions, but the young Dempseys were persuaded by a good friend to invest their proceeds, most of it conservatively, with the friend's asset management group in San Francisco.

As the market climbed for the next eighteen months, the Dempseys were content investors. Suddenly, their portfolio began to sink, along with the entire financial system, and they watched with alarm as their holdings seemed to evaporate. Through a maze of connections, they ended up in our office at Aureus in December 2008, after their stock account had lost nearly 40 percent of its value.

A CRISIS OF CONFIDENCE

The collapse of the financial markets was so fast and dramatic that the Dempseys could not believe how quickly their portfolio was evaporating. Luckily, they had a large cash position and numerous high-quality bonds, and together these made up more than half their portfolio. For the Dempseys, transferring their assets out of the hands of a good friend was traumatic, but leaving them in place was a more outsized risk than they could tolerate.

They made the decision to hire my firm. The account would be one of our largest. Considering what had happened to market values across our stock holdings, we were eager to win the business. When millions of people are watching their fortunes disappear, they generally are paralyzed into inaction, and very few prospects were knocking on our door.

Erin and Nick were, obviously, looking for someone they could trust. Despite owning many high-risk hedge funds and stocks, they were essentially conservative about their holdings, and had no debt of any type. Both were wary of the stock market, and Nick was particularly distrustful, in light of his dad's abrupt dismissal after decades with the same investment bank.

Nick wanted us to liquidate all their market-exposed holdings immediately, which would mean the widespread sale of much of the portfolio. We explained that we would research all the stocks, hedge funds, and illiquid investments they owned and get back to them soon with our recommendations. Our early risk was that Erin and Nick would not hire us unless we made clear our intention to include them in all decision making as we progressed with the account. To that end, we applied our experience working with families and our investing expertise, both of which, I believe, contributed to their decision to hire our firm.

We were eager for the Dempseys to trust us and take our advice. If, however, our suggestion was to retain stocks that they wanted to sell, we might lose their confidence. How far could we go before we jeopardized this new relationship? The Dempseys were hiring us to optimize their investments, and selling everything at once might not be the best solution, but we had little choice. They were suffering from their recent losses and would only feel comfortable or confident of our attentiveness if we eliminated all possible risk of them losing more now. After that, they expected, or at least hoped, that we would be skilled enough to presciently reinvest the proceeds when the market had bottomed. During periods of extreme negative sentiment, coinciding with market declines, almost all market strategists will be pessimistic. The financial press fuels such fear, wringing out more and more sellers who continue to depress prices as they rush for the exit. The point of extreme dejection, when there are no buyers in sight, is just about the time to buy again. The Dempseys were moving in that direction, squarely in a foxhole mentality, hiding from the shrapnel that they were sure would continue to fall around them.

By mid-January of 2009, when the market was down 43.8 percent from the October 2007 peak, we were popping Tums from indigestion, thinking about something stronger, but instead ensuring we purchased stocks with resilient value—picking among the rubble on days when we had the nerve. We feared that if we liquidated the Dempsey portfolio, it would be nearly impossible to convince them that it was time to buy again.

We worried about creating conflict with the Dempseys by pushing them too hard to keep some of the names in their account that we thought were very attractively priced after bottoming out from their declines, such as Microsoft, Lockheed Martin, Walmart, Abbott Laboratories, and Home Depot. If we did, we risked losing their trust and our brand-new account. We needed to find a balance between applying our best judgment about stock valuations and recognizing that this relationship was an important one to us and we did not want to risk jeopardizing it so soon.

We scaled back our plan on what stocks to keep, discussed our proposal with the Dempseys, who accepted our suggestions, and subsequently sold most of the stock holdings in the account before the end of January 2009, retaining only those in which we felt most confident. We redeemed their hedge fund holdings, both because of Nick's palpable fear concerning them, but also because we worried that several of these funds might be unable to pay out to all the shareholders demanding their money back.

The market confirmed the wisdom of Nick's "sell everything" strategy for the next six weeks, sliding another 24 percent from the time we opened the Dempsey account. The economy was a mess, the U.S. housing market was in free fall, the fate of the entire global financial structure was in limbo, and, as Tim Geithner stated, "The world economy is going through the most severe crisis in generations."[1] My friends in the business just called it a "shitstorm."

But every morning I reminded myself, in a reverie similar to that of people whose ship has capsized far offshore, that we were still hanging on and perhaps today was the day of our salvation. On March 6, 2009, the S&P 500 hit an intraday low of 666, which turned out to be the bottom—a whopping 57 percent drop from October 12, 2007.

Toward the end of March 2009, we decided that the timing was right to begin buying stocks in all the accounts we managed. This was a major shift from our most recent trading activity. For the past six months, we had been net sellers, divesting $138 of stock for every $100 we purchased. Stock valuations seemed expensive based on our concern that earnings estimates were too high for companies in many industries.

By the third week in March of 2009 we began to feel our stomachs settle a little. Maybe it was just that the weather was getting warmer in Boston and the days longer, but we were encouraged by the actions the Federal Reserve took to pump dollars into the economy and by the fact that the financial sector was still in business. Markets turn long before the fundamentals shift direction, and my partners and I were ready to make some bets that the world was not on the path to total financial annihilation. Our clients sign a contract that gives our firm discretion to make investment decisions in their accounts, but because of the extraordinary circumstances, we communicated with many of them before making any purchases. We were professional investors— our actions had an excellent chance of being right timed. We had very few dissents.

In contrast to our position as net sellers in the previous months, from March 6, 2009, until the end of the year, we purchased $136 worth of stock for each $100 that we sold, again not the most extreme sign of conviction, but a bet in the right direction. In our view, many companies were trading at extremely attractive prices that assumed their businesses would not recover for many years, a scenario that seemed overly dire. One of the lessons I learned decades ago, from Leo Dworsky, who managed Contrafund (one of the original Fidelity funds and now its largest) in the 1970s, was that you should always be uncomfortable with investment decisions because if they are obvious to everyone, you are way too late. Missing these opportunities meant we might be playing catch-up for many quarters. If we could not step up to the plate with the S&P down 50 percent from the peak and flickering signs of emerging economic light, we should get out of the business. In hindsight, those investment firms that did reinvest in early 2009 helped their relative performance and their business prospects considerably.

In the case of the Dempseys, my partner David and I flew out to visit them in person, making the case that we should start buying equities for them with the money we had raised. We showed them some analyses of stocks that were trading at very inexpensive multiples of their current earnings, with strong balance sheets, free cash flow, and ability to maintain their dividends.

After David and I explained why we thought that the stock market may have bottomed around February or early March, they both agreed that it was time to put some of the cash back to work. We decided to invest a 20 percent allocation, or around $10 million of the total $50 million, in stocks or equity-like assets.

WINNING STRATEGY, LOSING STRATEGY

In the context of risk-taking tenets, we thought we had right sized the scope, given the Dempseys' concerns about losing more money; right timed our purchases; and understood our clients' goals. Unfortunately, we were not cynical enough about the latter. David contacted the couple to confirm our market moves later that afternoon, because we did not want to begin the buying program for them without full approval, a move that was perhaps our undoing. To our surprise, we heard back from Erin the following afternoon, and she informed us that Nick was too worried to authorize our actions. He feared a terrorist attack, the failure of the Treasury's TARP program, runaway inflation, continued high unemployment, and the devastation of the entire consumer economy. That covered about everything; we would need to rethink our approach. She explained that they had lost so much money already that they could not face the prospect of losing any more.

We knew right then that we were in trouble. We were restricted by the Dempseys themselves from buying the stocks we were adding to all our other portfolios. We would underperform.

Nick reluctantly agreed weeks later to a smaller buying program. We struggled to gently push a higher allocation without jeopardizing the relationship. We talked on the phone, and wrote lengthy e-mails outlining why we should be buying more for them, but Nick would ask more questions, all reasonable, all signaling their apprehensions. By July, we were only 20 percent invested and tried to edge toward 25 percent. The market kept climbing higher.

In late September, less than nine months after we took over the account, we received our least favorite type of correspondence. The Dempseys had hired a large bank to serve as their custodian, replacing Fidelity, where we generally hold our assets. Now trust officers from the San Francisco office would be overseeing our actions. We suspected that the Dempseys were talking with friends who asked if their account had snapped back sharply since the bear market ended in March. The answer was no, but not by our design.

Since their account was still mostly in cash and fixed income, it had dramatically underperformed compared with more fully invested portfolios. Although we had been urging the Dempseys for months to invest more aggressively, we had been woefully unsuccessful at convincing Erin and Nick to go along with our program. Listening to the client, as I mentioned, is one key attribute in right sizing risk, but in this case, it was separating us from our investment strategy. The market was ascending, the Dempseys were refusing to let us invest their funds, and we might well take the blame.

When we met with the Dempseys in October to review their account, we pointed out that there was only a 15 percent allocation to equities, but the performance of those stocks, since inception, was up 207 percent![2] This was a result of what we had purchased and the handful of legacy holdings we had retained in the portfolio. We were ecstatic with the performance of the stocks, on the one hand, but acknowledged that the results for the entire account would have been much better if the stock weightings were higher.

In mid-October, we convened with the team from Monroe Bankcorp,* which now served as the custodian and was overseeing our results. The team was very critical of the limited equity proportion and the high percentage of cash and fixed income in the account, implying that this was our recommendation.

The Dempsey account was seriously at risk. Now we could lose the client through a conflict with the Monroe team, who clearly wanted to replace us and were eager to nail the underinvesting on our chests. Of course it didn't hurt that they were unencumbered by a sense of responsibility to defer to the Dempseys' intense fear of the market.

In January of 2010, we traveled back to the West Coast to meet with the Dempseys and review their accounts. Despite the fact that their stock return for 2009 grew 210 percent,[3] a number almost any manager would be proud of, they informed us they were moving the management of their account from Aureus to Monroe. They cited all sorts of reasons for their departure, such as their comfort level with a large institution (though they had moved from a much larger firm to us), the superior style of Monroe's reporting, and the high level of service.

With regard to service, we conducted many face-to-face meetings

---

* Monroe Bankcorp is a composite.

with the Dempseys, despite the distance, and spoke to them more frequently than to any other clients during that period. And at Aureus, unlike Monroe, the partners who meet with clients are also the investors, whose major function is to research and make portfolio decisions.

Erin and Nick never mentioned what I believed to be the true reason for their departure: the S&P 500 had risen 26 percent in 2009 and their entire account had grown only a modest 5 percent, mainly because it contained mostly cash and fixed income holdings, which at the time was a losing proposition.

The Dempseys were a flight risk from the very beginning unless we could be both very conservative in preserving their assets and very proactive in reinvesting the proceeds from the asset sales. It was impossible to do both. Once the attractive Monroe team of vice presidents powered up their colorful charts and presentations, our days were numbered.

In our approach to the Dempseys, we carefully considered the scope of their monetary loss and emotional trauma, offering lengthy meetings and calls to provide whatever conversation and support they required. This helped convince them that they should hire us at the end of 2008. For the following year, their account was very valuable to our firm, and I believe that we managed it the best way possible given our constraints.

What did work for us was the mere presence of the Dempsey account. After a horrendous 2008, they were a godsend. They arrived when our revenues might have declined in 2009, and I still appreciate that they came to us at a critical juncture in our firm's history. The viability of our company was never at risk, but we had no idea if some of our other clients would depart after being fed up with the gyrations of the market. Fortunately, the only relationship we lost in 2009 was the Dempseys. Perhaps if we had pushed harder, stressing our knowledge of markets and companies to advocate for increased market exposure, we might have prevailed, but I doubt that would have worked in the first half of 2009.

When looking at how we at Aureus and others consider risk, I now appreciate that we need to recognize the impact that severe monetary losses or emotional trauma can have on risk tolerance. In their way, the Dempseys were experiencing post-traumatic stress, as were many victims of the 2008 financial crisis. Their response reflected their defensiveness and an understandable suspicion of all financial advisors. Empathy and communication can improve the odds of connecting with people suffering from debilitating experiences, although sometimes our best efforts are not enough.

CHAPTER 8

Solving Puzzles

The manner in which Jeff Flowers and David Friend, Carbonite's founders, expanded beyond their well-tested software skills as they entered the small business market exemplifies sensible risk-taking. Sara Campbell, too, applied the tenets of sensible risk when she launched new retail stores as a destination for finished product that she was contractually obliged to produce. We have also seen how ignoring or violating those same tenets—as Genzyme did when it postponed construction of a new plant or as Sara Campbell did when she trusted Talbots's sales projections—can unravel years of solid strategic planning. We can observe how the tenets apply to the challenges facing a wide range of enterprises, despite the obvious differences among both the types of risk and the organizations.

The following chapter showcases several risk-related dilemmas. After posing the problem in the first several sections, we'll revisit the scenarios to observe the outcomes and how they might have been affected if the individual decision makers had properly evaluated the risks by applying the four tenets.

PUZZLE: GEORGE BELL AND EXCITE.COM

When George Bell accepted the job as CEO of Excite.com, an Internet portal and search engine, in 1996, he was a wildlife and adventure film-maker with deep experience in traditional media production. Although George was a Harvard-educated athlete with considerable energy, wit, and enthusiasm, he knew little about the Internet revolution he was being asked to join and help lead. He told me that he thought Kleiner Perkins, the venture capital powerhouse behind Excite, was the name of a law firm.

George Bell was not the only outsider moving into a starring role in this wild new world. The entire Internet was brand new, and there was no one already endowed with the technological, strategic, and marketing skills required for success. The managements of these new ventures, whether it was AOL, Yahoo, eBay, Lycos, or multitudes of others, were scrambling to grow as quickly as possible to preempt competition, grab the best talent available, close partnerships, ensure content for their websites, and promote like crazy.

The challenges for George were to focus on the correct market, right size the resources to capture and retain that business, and remain grounded in reality. The risk was that, without any definition or concept of what long-term success would look like in this arena, all the bushels of money investors were pouring into dot-com start-ups might not save them.

IVY INTEREST: HARVARD'S GAMBLE

In 2004, Larry Summers, president of Harvard University, participated in discussions with members of the ruling Harvard Corporation and his financial staff on how to finance the expansion of the Allston campus, across the Charles River from the central campus in Cambridge. Somehow, they reached a consensus to lock in the prevailing 4.7 percent interest rate for bonds that they would issue four years in the future to finance this new construction project. The vehicle that allows for future rate setting is called a "forward swap," arranged by investment banks that will exchange whatever rate Harvard would have incurred without the swap four years later with other borrowers. Swaps are not uncommon in debt financing, but both the $2.3 billion size and the four-year duration were very unusual.

This case has been covered in great detail by the press, although not from the perspective of the major participants and how they might have viewed the risk if interest rates turned down rather than moved upward as expected by almost all experts. I interviewed several people who were employed by Harvard at the time, most of whom spoke on condition of anonymity. It seems unlikely from my conversations that anyone in power was particularly worried that interest rates would plummet; if they were, they were afraid to voice that opinion and confront President Summers or his close allies on the swap proposal.

What is clear is that if the school were able to save 2 percent per year for thirty years on a $2.3 billion loan, that would represent $46 million a year or almost $1.4 billion over the life of the bond. However, Harvard and other institutions typically issued long-term bonds with a call provision, allowing the university to redeem the debt after a fixed number of years and issue it again at lower rates. So the benefit might be worth five or ten years' worth of lower interest payments, still a savings, but nothing close to $1.4 billion.

What would Harvard do if the direction of interest rates did not follow the script and climb over the next few years? This was the risk, however remote, that the administration might need to address.

TOXIC TO THE OFFICE: STARR AND A TROUBLED EMPLOYEE

No one would equate the risk of hedging billions in debt with the saga surrounding one employee at a regional real estate company, but the lessons about anticipating and reacting to risk are quite similar. When Steve Starr* hired Eve Ferrante† as the commercial leasing manager for his company in Austin, Texas, she had strong recommendations and appeared to have the requisite experience in the market. Starr Realty was growing quickly, and he was happy to have Eve.

Within six months, Steve realized something was amiss. There were irregularities in Eve's e-mails, missed appointments, and sloppy reports. In addition, Eve began to take very long lunch hours and behave erratically toward her colleagues. Steve took her to lunch to talk things over as well as to try a test that he had heard a friend describe as effective: let the other person drink whatever and however much she wants. You'll hear whatever is on her mind and will know if you're dealing with a problem drinker. Eve had too much to drink at lunch and expressed considerable enthusiasm for the fantastic waitstaff at a favorite after-work hangout near the office.

A few days later, Steve had dinner at the restaurant in question and asked the manager, who was a friend, if he saw Eve there often. Colin, the manager, told him that she was very well known there, and frequented the bar at lunch or after work several days a week.

When Steve reviewed Eve's work further, he discovered that she had failed to send contracts and related paperwork, jeopardizing several important deals. Steve took care of the problem but realized that his business's reputation could be irreparably harmed if Eve's negligence continued. When he confronted her, she became defensive about her behavior and disagreed that there were lapses in her work. Eve was not getting along with her colleagues or clients, she was irresponsible, and her work was unreliable—Steve knew that he had to let her go.

Steve's challenge was to separate Eve from Starr Realty without her causing much damage. Based on comments she'd made around the office, he felt it likely that Eve would sue for gender discrimination.

---

* Steve Starr is a composite.
† Eve Ferrante is a composite.

When he told his attorney about the situation, his lawyer agreed that the sooner Steve let her go, the better. He was not going to allow Eve's problems at work destroy his company.

The risks ranged from the possibility that Eve's unreliability would damage the business if she stayed on, to her potential retaliation upon dismissal. Steve feared a long and expensive lawsuit that would surely impact his reputation, budget, and time. He needed to decide what to do.

HACKED AWAY: INTERNET FRAUD

Like every new business, Aureus faced many hurdles in the first years, and we tried to apply a practical approach to these. Having seen many friends, colleagues, and acquaintances start all types of financial services companies, I had the opportunity to watch and learn from their successes and failures. I had not yet clearly identified the four tenets that I now apply to risk.

The goal of every financial services firm is to have enough assets under management that the fees more than cover expenses, including the salaries of the founders. The primary way to attract additional clientele is through strong performance. The biggest mistake I saw repeatedly was entrepreneurs creating a high-cost infrastructure before growing their revenues sufficiently to cover such expenses. Short-term, weak results due to a market slump or poor stock or investment selection would hurt the top line, and if the fixed costs were too high, the firm might never even cross that breakeven level.

David and I expected to take no salary for the first year, or maybe two. We right sized our rent and office space, which is very expansive and beautifully built, thanks to our landlord. The cornerstone tenant had left the building three years earlier, leaving 75 percent of the space vacant, and our landlord was desperate. In addition, we right sized our initial headcount, our market data services, trading and custody platform, and all our other service providers, once we sorted out our initial misstep with a very high-priced corporate law firm.

Fortunately, our formation allowed us to capture three more strong years in global stock markets. That was lucky, of course, but the economy was strong and both David and I felt that the momentum, over the next few years, was in our favor. Our collective experience among the original partners was in managing stock portfolios and, to a lesser extent, alternative investments, such as hedge funds. We diligently learned all about compliance, followed all the rules implicitly, and developed procedures for trading, reporting, security, and client service.

As for skepticism, my middle name should be "cynical." At Fidelity, I learned that the great investors have tremendous capacity to visualize incredible new concepts, products, and services for the companies in which they invest, but they are always intensely clear on every detail of the model illustrating the road to such lofty goals. There is no unbridled optimism without deep inquiry and analysis.

The second way to grow and retain business in our industry is to develop a reputation for competence in all aspects of client service. In 2011, despite all our attention to process and execution, we hit a speed bump with damaging force. We manage assets for very wealthy people and sometimes they spend a bit of money. A large number of our clients have us send regular distributions from their accounts, but occasionally they ask for sums outside the norm—these may be for a charitable donation or a major purchase for themselves or a family member.

It was, therefore, not particularly noteworthy when Nicole,* our director of client services, received an e-mail from Christine,† a long-term customer who travels extensively, explaining that she needed funds for a few large Asian antiques while she was traveling in the Far East. They exchanged e-mails, and Christine sent Nicole the wiring instruc-

---

* Nicole is a pseudonym.
† Christine is a pseudonym.

tions to a bank in South Korea from which Christine could access the cash; then Nicole loaded the transfer and hit "send."

Almost immediately, Nicole received another e-mail from Christine, thanking her but also mentioning that she had found some other beautiful items to purchase and needed another wire. At this point, Nicole got goose bumps, and had what she later described as an "Oh shit!" moment, when she realized that she had perhaps been duped by a hacker.

Nicole ran to my office and recounted the story, and I asked her to show me the e-mails from "Christine," who it seemed increasingly unlikely was our client. Upon careful reading, it was clear to me that the writer was not a native English-speaking person, but Nicole had many quick e-mails from Christine over the years about purchases in different parts of the world, sometimes hastily written, and she had not noticed the improper grammar. We called David to join us and placed a call to Christine, asking her to call me right away, then called Fidelity, our custodian, to see if the transfer had gone through (of course it had!), if they could intercept it before the recipient withdrew the money (already gone!), and if they would call their contacts at the FBI (they would, but good luck!).

We needed to decide immediately what to do when Christine called back. We had to tell her the truth, of course, and inform her she needed to change her e-mail password immediately. However, we had just wired a large amount of money into cyberspace and had to make that right. I needed a few minutes of quiet to think about the risks of different actions, so I asked Nicole to stay in touch with Fidelity for any news, and I would have my decision very soon.

TRYING TO SOLVE THE PUZZLE: GEORGE BELL AND EXCITE.COM

For George Bell, the most critical risk was in choosing the direction for Excite. The explosion of the Internet made it very difficult to predict which model would succeed, and euphoria abounded wherever you looked. He and the venture capitalists who had helped fund the enterprise ultimately bet on building a portal and search engine. The search space was jammed with competitors, among them AltaVista, AOL, Yahoo, Infoseek, HotBot, Magellan, Lycos, WebCrawler, and Ask Jeeves. Most of them no longer exist.

The dominant player, as we now know, became Google, because its technology, superior to that of its predecessors, produced search results so accurately and quickly that it became the most popular. Famously, Sergey Brin and Larry Page, two Stanford students who founded Google, offered their company to Excite for $1 million in 1999, but George, in a decision that may always haunt him, declined. He was intent on preserving the cohesive Excite culture, which he felt would be disrupted by a Google acquisition.

In hindsight, the risk to Excite's culture would probably have been worth taking, at least by one measure, based on Google's current market value of over $360 billion. However, it was almost impossible, in the late 1990s, to quantify the scope of risk in this environment because of the insatiable demand by investors who bid up the prices daily on Internet public companies. George acquired competitors Magellan and Webcrawler with Excite stock and built a large campus of buildings to house the expanding Excite workforce. In early 1999, he accepted a $7 billion offer from @Home, a high-speed Internet service provider that partnered with cable companies such as ATT and Comcast, keeping a third of the monthly subscription fee. George was asked by the controlling board to become CEO of the recently merged companies, and he agreed.

The most significant tenet that Excite (as well as hundreds of other web start-ups) violated was lack of skepticism. As George Bell describes it, those in the industry were all undiluted optimists who believed that ad revenue would mushroom, cable deals would expand exponentially, and business growth was in the very early innings.

Nearly all participants—whether they were the executives of

dot-com companies, mutual fund and hedge fund managers, or typical Americans watching their 401(k) statements—trusted the forecasts. The stocks surged every day, which seemed to be ample proof. Unfortunately, virtually none of the forecasts made by companies or analysts in 1999 became reality in the next few years.

At its peak, Excite@Home was worth nearly $35 billion in market value, with revenues of more than $600 million but an annual loss of $7.4 million. As a comparison, Colgate, Comcast, and United Technologies all traded at market capitalizations in the same region but had sales upward of $9 billion, $8 billion, and $26 billion, respectively, with net profit between $1 billion and $2 billion each.

During this bubble, companies such as Excite needed to keep expanding ahead of their competitors, adding people, acquisitions, and offices, but it was unclear where the strategy was leading. The pace of megadeals and acquisitions in 2000 barely allowed anyone time to safely jump off the ramp of the private jet and into the limo. Excite@Home was a victim and a participant in this land grab.

When Yahoo partnered with Google to power its search engine, however, it handed Google the keys to the search empire. Players across the industry were battling for dominance in their niche.

Excite@Home initially held an unassailable position as the provider of broadband services to the cable companies; however, a major regulatory issue, referred to as open access, began to send shudders through the cable industry. The FCC conducted hearings on whether broadband availability should be treated as a public utility rather than through exclusive contracts. Although open access was never legislated at the federal or state level, the presumption was that Excite@Home's pricing structure would be challenged, undercutting the value of its franchise. The cable companies swiftly began offering their own broadband packages, bypassing Excite@Home.

George Bell needed to differentiate his company's service, but he became increasingly frustrated by the intrusive directives from executives at the company's cable customers. The backdrop of a crash of the technology and Internet stocks made his efforts much less likely to succeed. He decided to leave the firm in April of 2001 and move back to the East Coast with his family. George's replacement was Patti Hart, a longtime veteran of the telecom industry, with close ties to ATT and other service providers. Excite@Home's stock plummeted from a peak of $128 per share to $1 within two years, amid the Chapter 11 bankruptcy filing that occurred more than a year after George Bell had departed.

Excite@Home never exploited a unique expertise to preempt competition. Perhaps it could have developed a lock on a market, as Amazon, eBay, Yelp, TripAdvisor, Priceline, or PayPal had done, but the young creators of the Excite portal were innovators, competing concurrently with a handful of other groups, all aiming to attract new web users to their site.

Even if George Bell and his team had been skeptical of their own forecasts, it is not clear that they would have identified a new direction or prospered if they'd pursued it. Since returning to the Boston area, George has been CEO of two companies, his tenure at both ending with the successful sale of the enterprise. In addition, he has been a partner at General Catalyst, a venture capital firm.

SWAP OUTCOMES: HARVARD'S GAMBLE

The Harvard treasurer's office kept a careful watch on the value of the swaps they had placed to ensure the 4.72 percent rate on over $2 billion of debt the university would issue four years into the future. Although long-term rates did inch over 5 percent briefly in 2006 and 2007, they began to slide in 2008, and then simply crashed to around 2.5 percent as a postscript to the demise of Lehman Brothers, Bear Stearns, and numerous other financial institutions.

Most borrowers would be thrilled with a weak interest rate environment, but Harvard had locked itself into a 4.7 percent borrowing cost for a very large absolute quantity of debt. In addition, the school had allocated 80 percent of its cash reserves, or $6 billion, to be invested with the Harvard endowment, another decision that defies right-sizing principles, considering that this is a school with massive, fixed operating costs. That bet was also crumbling, and Harvard authorities, gripped by panic at the end of 2008, chose to terminate the swap agreements and buy them back from J. P. Morgan, among other banks, for close to $1 billion over the next few weeks. Considering the already disastrous period for banks, this could have been their best business, by far, of the holiday season.

Rather than dissect why Harvard so cavalierly played these odds, it is worth considering the tenets as they apply to this case. No one involved with the decisions at the time has explained who exactly pushed for the size of the swap trade or the cash investment, which lost $1.8 billion by early 2009, and then pulled the trigger on both.

The sheer size of the swap, at $2.3 billion, was larger than Harvard or, probably, any university had ever issued previously. Given the uncertainly about the interest rate outcome, this was too large a bet, in the opinion of several economists and endowment managers with whom I spoke. Such an aggressive approach suggests arrogance, which can be harmless in small doses but often dangerous in larger ones. The four-year horizon was also much longer than that of typical swaps.

Larry Summers, the university's president at the time, is a distinguished economist. Among his colleagues and advisers were fixed income experts at Harvard Management Company, Harvard Business School, and even the Harvard Corporation. However, they had no experience with the size and duration of this swap instrument. As trained academics and practitioners, they were well aware that predictions about bond rates several years in the future are very likely to be wrong.

The Harvard power elite, including Larry Summers, believed that the bond market would fall, rates would rise, and the value of the Harvard endowment would continue to climb. The models supporting these predictions were meticulously developed, highly complex, and incorrect. There was probably not enough skepticism about these models applied to the discussion before putting on the swaps as well a flawed understanding of the extent of possible damage to the university on such a large bet.

Even when the swap value plummeted and the corporation chose to repurchase and unwind the option, its timing was off. A few months later the cost would have been hundreds of millions less.

RESTORING PEACE: STARR AND A TROUBLED EMPLOYEE

Though he was looking at a risk on a scale much smaller than that of the Harvard gamble, Steve Starr knew that he needed to let his commercial leasing manager, Eve Ferrante, go. She was unreliable, a problem drinker, and difficult with coworkers.

Steve orchestrated a meeting for the two of them in his office. After one sentence, she knew she was being fired, and let loose a string of profanities worthy of any construction crew, grabbed whatever she wanted in her office, and told Steve he'd be sorry. Two weeks later, Steve received notice from Eve's attorneys that Starr Realty was being sued for several forms of discrimination. He met with his firm's lawyer to discuss their strategy.

Eve was seeking a huge amount in damages. She had no case, but Steve needed to consider the potential downside. Her attorney was probably on a contingency, but Steve would be paying out of pocket and the legal bills could grow out of control. His firm's reputation could be hurt for years to come. Importantly, this case could consume considerable time and energy, resources that were already in short supply.

Steve needed to right size the case and determine the most he should pay to settle. As a married mother of three, Eve, he assumed, was not anxious for anything to come to light about her poor judgment or lunchtime and after-work habits. The right timing of a settlement was as soon as possible. He was sure that Eve had nothing up her sleeve to throw at him; she was the one with spotty attendance, lack of follow-through, and a toxic attitude.

Steve's lawyer made an offer that was slightly more than he wanted to pay but much less than the expense of a protracted court case. She took the money, and Starr Realty escaped with its reputation intact and its collegial office culture restored.

VOICE CONFIRMATION: INTERNET FRAUD

I sat in my office with the door closed, deciding what to tell Christine, the client from whose account we had mistakenly wired a six-figure amount (low six figures, honestly) to a thief, most likely in Asia. I remember looking at the clock on my phone, putting my head in my hands, and then two minutes later looking at it again.

I called David and told him that we needed to refund Christine's account fully with our company's cash reserves. He agreed that it was the right thing to do. We have always maintained a large cash balance just in case something unexpected happened, and now it had. If we recovered the funds, Aureus would keep them, but the chance of that was quickly dwindling to less than my likelihood of hitting the lottery. Christine would think much more highly of us this way than if we waited, and there was no reason to wait. If she decided we were idiots and pulled her account, she would not think less of us if we refunded her lost assets immediately.

No insurance company will cover hacked funds other than at a premium that makes the coverage irrelevant, and the fine print, which Stacey, my longtime assistant, and I read after this event, exempts claims for theft originating in many developing countries and most of Asia.

I called Christine and she picked up this time, having just heard my voice mail asking her to call me. I explained exactly what happened, and that we were refunding her account the exact amount lost on that day. We spoke for a short while longer, as I suspect Christine was in as much shock as I was, and I assured her that we were going to review and change our procedures for wiring funds to prevent this from ever happening again. She thanked me and we hung up. It was unclear whether Christine would stay with us or not.

Computer hacking is a thriving industry, and we were easily duped in a well-known scam. Despite our embarrassment, I am sharing this story because so many other companies have been the victim of hacking; I feel slightly less stupid in the company of major corporations like Target, Visa, and Anthem, as well as various branches of the U.S. government. However, we should already have instituted tighter rules about distributions from accounts.

We had been blind to the significant risk posed by the possible hacking of a client's e-mail. Our policies about wiring assets changed that day, and now require a phone call and voice confirmation for any withdrawal of $5,000 or greater that is not a standing distribution for that account. Most banks and investment firms now have similar restrictions. These rules may be inconvenient, but they represent an appropriate safeguard.

Hopefully, the measure we have in place across the assets under our care will protect us against the next cyber attack. We have improved our diligence and security systems, and know our custodians have done the same.

Christine was appreciative of the rapid steps we took to reimburse her account, and has referred other clients to us. We applied right timing to the risk of further damaging our reputation and I have never regretted that move. The FBI investigation failed to uncover more than one vague lead, which was disappointing but not unexpected. Christine's confidence in our firm confirms that we acted correctly to manage one risk, even though we totally failed to control another.

Major decisions at businesses or nonprofit organizations must include an evaluation of the scope of the exposure and the time frame involved. We must know as much as possible about the marketplace, the participants, and the customers, while remaining skeptical about research that seems overly optimistic or simplistic. None of this is easy, particularly in the heat of a crisis, which is often when we are forced to make our most important decisions. However, keeping in mind a framework to address risk can help assuage those challenges.

PART 3

Investing

CHAPTER 9

The Bubble

The stock market is a great equalizer. Those of us who live, work, and play its daily game have great respect for its power or we simply do not last. My career as a fund manager and analyst has shaped my understanding of risk and the way we can appraise its elements. The examples throughout this chapter highlight some of the most interesting people I have worked with as well as lessons gleaned from my life in the market. I'll also outline the role of sensible risk-taking in addressing the market.

I am not much for hyperbole, but the period between early February and late March of 2000 was among the worst of my life. The new millennium arrived benevolently, amid quickly dissipated Y2K fears that preyed on the possibility that systems from traffic lights to global banking networks would crash. Little did we know that a different type of crash was imminent, one caused by the blatant disregard of sensible risk-taking. The 1999 Internet-dominated bull market carried into the opening weeks of 2000, at which point most of us were somewhere on the spectrum from euphoric to bewildered.

Even those of us who recognized the insanity of the tech bubble could not help but glow a tiny bit with our own participation in, and even contribution to, the strongest market surge in our lifetime. Through 1999 and into the early days of the new millennium, numerous stocks jumped 10 percent a day with regularity. Investors poured money into our funds at Fidelity quicker than you can say "401(k)," and it was our duty to put that money to work. With greater sums invested, however, your position becomes even more vulnerable to the effects of a downturn.

The funds I managed eclipsed $10 billion that year as I outperformed my benchmark. However, life is more than your last quarterly results (although it doesn't always seem so). My mother had been sick for several years with a neurological condition that manifested very much like Lou Gehrig's disease, but with the devastating-sounding name of multiple system atrophy (MSA). I tried to visit her every day on my way home from work, arriving home much later than was ideal for my four teenage children.

My mother-in-law had likewise just been diagnosed with a very aggressive form of lymphoma, and by early February of that year, the prognosis looked dire. On several visits to Massachusetts General Hospital, I recounted the wild leaps of stocks such as Yahoo, Broadcom, and AOL to my father-in-law. I described the gravity-defying action of the tech and biotech stocks, along with their unrealistic prices, but I was reluctant to sell them for fear of losing performance relative to my benchmark and competition. There appeared to be more risk assigned to not owning these companies in my fund than to holding them despite their very high valuation.

DISREGARDING SENSE

Everything has a value, however, and many of us, as investors, lost our reason and sense of discipline in the midst of tech's unprecedented ascendance. Not only did we allow Internet stocks to grow in our portfolios beyond a reasonable size relative to their earnings, but we forgot our years of training in analyzing the value of our equity holdings. In our enthusiasm to be a part of the world-changing rise of the digital age, we clearly forgot about right sizing our commitment and about considering the time it might take for these new firms to generate the profits implied in their stock prices. Unforgivably, we also blindly accepted the projections that companies and analysts had presented as gospel.

The technology sector in 1999 accounted for nearly 30 percent of the market capitalization of the S&P 500, but only 15 percent of its profits. Because market prices anticipate the future, the implication was that tech earnings would double their weight of total market income over the next decade, thereby justifying their premium. If the percentage of S&P 500 earnings accounted for by tech in 2015 were roughly 30 percent, we might conclude that the bet made in 1999 was appropriate, and investors had right sized their positioning.

However, in 2015, technology company earnings as a percentage of the total S&P are approximately 20 percent, far below the 30 percent value allotted to the group more than fifteen years ago. Despite the phenomenal success of Apple, Google, and Facebook, investors remain wary after losing so much money in the meltdown of the new millennium.

One of the Internet's earliest darlings was Yahoo, Inc., a name with which most Americans were once familiar, but which is now thought of by millennials as a home for fantasy football and as a secondary search vehicle. In 1999 alone, Yahoo stock climbed 265 percent, placing it at number 20 on the list of top performers in the Nasdaq 100 for the year.

During the site's early years, I met with the management of Yahoo many times, beginning with CEO Tim Koogle, who visited the Fidelity office during Yahoo's initial public offering (IPO) roadshow. We loved the company and its concept of transitioning from a web directory to a full-service digital media behemoth offering one-stop shopping for search, content, communications, and commerce. Institutions from Fidelity to California's state pension plan, most hedge funds, and individual investors swallowed all the rhetoric and gobbled up more and more shares. Yahoo's price catapulted from $33 at the beginning of 1998 to $175 only two years later.

By early 2000, Yahoo's market value or capitalization was over $70 billion, with annual revenues of approximately $1 billion and net earnings of $71 million. The worth of Yahoo was, therefore, seventy times its sales and about a thousand times its net income, ratios that revealed wild enthusiasm even in an era of huge expectations.

Obviously, Yahoo and a host of other web-based market darlings traded at stratospheric levels on the belief that they would grow into their prices. Even the Warburg Dillon Read analysts, despite a buy rating on the stock at $353 in January of 2000, were questioning the validity of their own numbers.[1] They discounted expected 2005 sales ($4.2 billion) and earnings ($1.3 billion) back five years and "applying a multiple of 100 times to our discounted EPS estimate and 25 times to our discounted revenue estimate, arrived at a price target of approximately $155," a price that was 56 percent lower than the stock was trading at the time! Ten years later, Yahoo's revenues barely surpass this 2005 estimate, and its 2015 net income forecast from a Cantor Fitzgerald report dated May 20, 2015, of $364 million is 72 percent below the earlier projection.[2]

Only a sustained period of annual net income growth exceeding 100 percent would justify the price Yahoo's stock traded for in early 2000. In fact, the company's earnings growth between 2000 and 2015 was around 13 percent per year, far from a triple-digit number. Although 13 percent per year for a fifteen-year period is outstanding, it cannot adequately support three hundred times earnings per share, which means that the momentum propelling it forward will eventually stop or reverse.

A Credit Suisse report opined that Yahoo was so attractive because "We believe that Yahoo is playing in a larger sandbox (than AOL, eBay, Lycos and CNET, as examples) with favorable economics that could justify a steeper premium."[3] Steeper than Everest? Reading that opinion now, I find it slightly depressing to reflect on how gullible I was at the time, failing to rely on what I could grasp as attainable and recognize what I knew was outrageous.

On February 18, 2000, my mother-in-law, Anita Firestone, died. My mother, coincidentally also named Anita, who had the same birthday as Anita F., but, at seventy-three, was a few years younger, mourned the loss of her friend and felt that she herself should have been the one to die. On March 1, her caregiver, Miriam, called me at work to say that my mother had suffered a seizure. When I learned that they were heading by ambulance to St. Elizabeth's Hospital in Boston, I immediately left the office.

The market was spiking again that day. The growth-oriented Nasdaq 100 Index closed on March 1 at 4,784, an incredible 43 percent higher than its opening point a mere three months earlier. As the taxi pulled up to the entrance of the hospital, I called Bob Durkin, my trader at Fidelity, and told him that if I had guts I would start aggressively selling all my tech, biotech, and Internet stocks. He asked, "What do you want to do?" to which I replied, "I just can't make any decisions about stocks right now."

There was no cell reception inside St. Elizabeth's, so I signed off and walked through the revolving hospital doors. Ever since that day, I have regarded my inaction as the greatest mistake of my career. On March 2, 2000, my mother passed away, less than two weeks after my husband's mother. I cannot blame my failure to sell some of the most expensive stocks in my fund on my own personal dilemma, but when I remember that crazy market period, I think of this terrible day.

Once Yahoo enlisted Google to power its search engine, it lost any chance of dominating its consumers' navigation process. The company never became a controlling factor in any major sphere of revenue-generating content, such as Amazon, first for books and then for everything else; eBay for auctions; Priceline for travel; and Ticketmaster for concert tickets. While consumers have used Yahoo extensively through the years to follow finance news and fantasy sports, they do not pay for those experiences, and advertising revenues have fallen well short of the long-term forecasts.

So has Yahoo stock. In mid-2015, Yahoo's market value was

$38.5 billion, with $4.3 billion in estimated sales and $323 million in consensus earnings for 2015. According to Yahoo's 2014 annual report, its holding of the Chinese e-commerce site Alibaba was valued at approximately $40 billion, implying a negative worth for the remainder of the company.

It was not a mistake to own Yahoo for its first three years of existence. Trends, as George Vanderheiden, one of the best Fidelity fund managers ever, told me, are much more durable than you ever expect. Playing the dot-com stocks during the 1997 to 1999 period was essential to competitiveness. However, when the bubble expanded and its size overwhelmed the rest of the stock market, and when intelligent analysts spouted projections about monetizing eyeballs that both sounded silly and defied logic, we should have realized that the party was almost over. When it ended, the crash was earsplitting. Yahoo cascaded relentlessly to below $5 per share in the wake of 9/11.

DAWNING LIGHT

For many months, I reran the reel of my phone conversation with Bob Durkin, when I almost but not quite made an important and bold move. I ignored two tenets of sensible risk-taking that would have aided my situation: relying on my knowledge and remaining skeptical.

If I could not convince myself that the expected revenue and profits were realistic or I could not come close to the vision of the companies or the Wall Street firms promoting these stocks, I should have walked away. Because I discounted my experience and training, and suspended my skepticism, I owned too many of these frothy positions.

Fortunately, reason kicked in before the bottom, as I was able to sell with some dignity intact, but not nearly as soon as I should have. I have always blamed myself for any portfolio mistakes, resisting the temptation to blame a company or its management for poor performance, as is common in my business. No one at AOL, JDS Uniphase, Siebold, BEA Systems, Human Genome Sciences, or Millennium Pharmaceuticals forced me to own their stock in the downturn. The choice falls entirely to the decision makers.

If I had to characterize my trading style, I would say that I buy and sell early. However, selling prematurely was a loser's game in 1998 and 1999; the stocks just kept plowing ahead. I had experienced phenomenal stock appreciation years earlier as the first cable and cellular stock analyst at Fidelity, witnessing with awe, but also understanding, how industries could lose hundreds of millions while their stock values skyrocketed. The cable and mobile phone corporations eventually began to practically coin money after years of heavy investing in their infrastructure. Patience paid off.

Perhaps these dot-com businesses would follow a path similar to that of Comcast and Cellular Communications? But in my heart I knew there were intrinsic differences. The cable and cell phone companies had monthly annuity streams from their growing customer base, while most of the Internet and biotech darlings of the late 1990s had no real chance of meaningful sales or profitability for years.

Not only did I disregard my analytical ability as I docilely accepted very aggressive projections, I became caught in a game of chicken. If I sold too many of the high flyers before my competition did, and the stocks kept climbing, I would lose valuable relative performance. The idea that I thought I could time my exit once the building started burning is laughable.

CLEVER EXIT

Jennifer Uhrig was more cynical than I was regarding exposure to overpriced stocks. One of the most talented mutual fund managers I know, Jennifer quickly rose through the analyst ranks at Fidelity to become the first Mid Cap Fund manager, in large part because it was her idea. Never a shrinking violet, Jennifer stated her mind, usually very clearly, but was also known for her self-deprecating sense of humor. In early 1997, Abby Johnson, the daughter of Fidelity's chairman, was responsible for fund assignments, and she asked Jennifer to take over management of both the $10 billion held in the VIP Growth Fund and the Advisor Equity Growth Fund.

If you notice, I didn't say Jennifer was one of the most talented women in the business, because that would severely shortchange her expertise. Jennifer probably does hold the record for the most mutual fund assets managed solely by one woman, but anyone handling more than $35 billion, which she has, is in rarified territory already. She is a professional who knows how to apply right sizing and right timing to major investment decisions.

All funds and portfolios managed for individuals or institutions have a benchmark against which their performance is compared. We fund managers become addicted to beating our benchmark and our competition within our category. If asked confidentially, nearly all fund managers would rather be down 1 percent for a quarter when the benchmark is off 3 percent than up 1 percent when their index is ahead 3 percent. We play a game of relative performance, which is how we sell to new customers.

Those of us who are engaged in actively managing mutual funds or stock portfolios believe that we can apply our knowledge of companies and markets to beat our index. This style is called "active management," while the process of owning stocks in line with the benchmark's weightings is referred to as "passive management." Adherents to the latter believe in the efficient markets theory and reject the idea that anyone can outperform a benchmark over time, essentially because markets are very efficient.

Active managers, such as Jennifer Uhrig and I, believe that there is considerable inefficiency in stock pricing, which creates opportunities to buy equities before the "market" recognizes that they are mispriced. The debate over active versus passive management has raged for decades and is beyond the scope of this book. Despite being a purebred stock picker, I recognize the tremendous value of index funds, and we own them in selective accounts at our firm.

It is fair to say, however, that many firms with a mandate to actively select stocks harbor professionals whom many of us call "index huggers." This term refers to people who cling to their benchmark or index. My colleagues and I have often referred to these closet indexers as "wimps" who have no spine or conviction in their choices. Generally, after fees are deducted, they trail their benchmark. While they may stay within a tight performance range in their index by not taking any risk of over-weighting or underweighting a position—or even, perish the thought, owning a stock that is not in the index—they can never strongly outperform. What's the fun in that?

Jennifer Uhrig's benchmark was the Russell 3000 Growth index, compiled by the Russell Consulting Group, an index that contains the stocks within the 3000 name composite with higher earnings momentum than the "value" segment. In 1999, tech companies already made up a hefty 50 percent of the index, a level roughly approximate to Jennifer's, but the Russell administrators, invoking the requirements to reflect changes in constituents' market values, raised the technology weighting to 60 percent at the peak of the Internet mania, in 2000.

As most fund managers will admit, sector bets are often the driving force of relative returns. Just ask anyone stuck with a double weighting in energy stocks during the fourth quarter of 2014, when the price of crude oil collapsed over 50 percent. So, in mid-2000, when Jennifer's benchmark weight in tech jumped to 60 percent, she faced a critical challenge: should she follow the benchmark higher, or hold steady with her current positioning in stocks related to search, web, browser, online, enterprise, infrastructure, software, and fiber optics?

SOFT ON VISION

Among the beloved technology firms of the late 1990s was the software firm BroadVision, which developed and sold software applications to clients to create their own e-commerce platforms. Its stock was number two on the list of top-performing Nasdaq names of 1999, up a mind-blowing 1,494 percent that year.[4] BroadVision represents a fascinating case of an enterprise for which the analyst community and investors simultaneously dismissed all conceivable cynicism about future growth projections.

The market believed that there was an immediate need for every entity from the *New York Times* to Target to build an attractive, user-friendly, and interactive website, subsequently requiring sizable investments. BroadVision was an early entrant and leader in this category. The firm went public in 1996, rapidly becoming one of the stars in the Internet orbit, and commanded an enterprise value of $10 billion at its peak in March of 2000.[5]

With expectations for 2000 of $140 million in sales and $18 million in profits, investors declared that each dollar of BroadVision's sales was worth over $70, and each dollar of earnings worth $550. A Deutsche Bank report from September of 1999 cites International Data Corporation (IDC) estimates of more than $1 trillion in global Internet commerce sales by 2003.[6] Just seeing numbers like that in print should have raised a red flag so bright that we would think twice before pushing the buy button.

In 1999, when the Deutsche Bank report was written, the value of all retail sales in the United States, including cars and food, which were unlikely to be e-commerce purchases by 2003, was nearly $3 trillion.[7] The compound growth rate of retail spending over the previous eight years had been 5.5 percent, and there was no reason to believe this would change dramatically, even if Americans migrated their purchasing online. If the retail growth rate nearly doubled to 10 percent annually for three years, the total in 2003 would reach $4.4 trillion, of which $1 billion would represent close to a quarter of retail sales.

It was my inclination at the time to determine whether this was even remotely realistic. For example, consider that the e-commerce share of U.S. retail in 2000 was negligible, at less than 1 percent of all purchases.[8] BroadVision may have signed American Airlines, Walmart, Home Depot, and Citibank as customers, but the websites of these companies were hardly operational and development was lengthier and more complicated than anyone expected.

When IDC made its bold forecast that global Internet sales would hit $1 trillion in three years, the number of e-commerce transactions in the U.S. was only $56 billion. The level of growth expected was totally unrealistic and cried out for skepticism.

In fact, the $1 trillion milestone was not reached until nearly a decade later, in 2012.[9] The U.S. total online sales for 2014 were $300 billion, representing only about a quarter of the world's volume.[10] Although we may think that we buy "everything" online, domestic Internet sales represent merely 7 percent of our total retail purchases according to U.S. government data.[11] Further confounding such seemingly wild forecasts, total retail demand including food grew much slower than anticipated, at nearly 3 percent over the past decade.

Given such statistics, what happened to BroadVision is not surprising. There was abundant competition to provide website software, weaker than expected prices, fewer than anticipated buyers, and higher than desired operating costs. The stock price simply imploded.

BroadVision still exists today, but its current market capitalization is only $28 million, a small fraction of the $10 billion that once excited investors to near madness. The stock was delisted in 2006, both because it could not pay its debt commitments and because the share price fell to a level the Nasdaq considered unsustainable. In mid-2015, BVSN was once again listed, trading at $5.70, a shadow of its former self—which, adjusted for stock splits, was $19,368 per share at its peak in March of 2010!

BroadVision's value was based on misplaced belief in wildly aggressive forecasts about the e-commerce market and the firms that would pay to create elaborate websites in the near term. This was clear when buyers failed to apply any real skepticism before diving into the feeding frenzy themselves. It made no sense to project that a quarter of retail purchases in 2003 would be transacted online, when most retailers were still just thinking about creating a web presence. The percentage of Americans with smartphones, one of the key drivers of e-commerce sales, did not surpass 25 percent until 2009. Finally, there was insufficient infrastructure for shipping such an amazing influx of packages.

The implicit size of the e-commerce demand embedded in BroadVision stock in 2000 defied logic. The timing expectation was far too optimistic for the build out of consumer-facing Internet platforms, in large part due to unrealistic projections. Also, BroadVision may not have had the right skill set to satisfy the market and address the complex software needs of its clients, as the company underestimated both the rapidly shifting landscape and the abilities of its competitors.

DOWNSIZE—OUTPERFORM

Jennifer Uhrig wisely chose not to chase the benchmark. Her reasons are reflected in several practical risk-taking tenets, the most important of which was the sheer size of a sector bet in a supposedly diversified fund. According to Jennifer, a pragmatist as well as a forward thinker, she already had nearly half her fund in technology. The tech-heavy Nasdaq Composite Index had soared over 300 percent since Fed chairman Alan Greenspan highlighted the "irrational exuberance" driving the market, suggesting that his timing of the top was more than slightly off. As Jennifer told me, "Everyone who was talking about the absurd valuations of stocks for two years and sold early was either out of a job or about to lose one."

There were already signs in the spring of 2000 that the icing was sliding off the cake. Nokia, one of the key horsemen of the tech/telecom stampede, missed its second-quarter estimate, and its stock sank 20 percent. The Nasdaq had peaked at 5,048 intraday on March 10. As a point of reference, more than fifteen years later, the Nasdaq 100 Index, which reached 4,360 on July 9, 2015, had yet to recover to that level. Jennifer's assets under management had ballooned to $38 billion from $10 billion in early 1997. Underweighting technology by 10 percent meant owning $4 billion less of that sector than the index.

Jennifer was really betting that tech stocks would drop in value and that her competition would not move to the 60 percent technology weighting. She was increasingly nervous about wildly ambitious projections by CEOs who seemed to take their "Masters of the Universe" status seriously. The prevalence of this attitude was on full display when I watched as the billionaire (on paper, anyway) CEO of a Silicon Valley high-speed chip company screamed uncontrollably at a waiter in the Ritz-Carlton Hotel in San Francisco because the lettuce in his sandwich was too "soggy."

The devastation was astounding. The Nasdaq, which had realized tremendous gains between January 1, 1999, and March 10, 2000, plummeted 84 percent over the course of the next thirty-one months. Not only was it clear that the emperors in tech and biotech had no clothes (and they were almost all men, with eBay's Meg Whitman one of the few exceptions, and that company that did have some clothes), but then 9/11 destroyed whatever shaky confidence had reemerged since the downfall.

Jennifer's fund outperformed impressively during this period because she had been appropriately cynical of the projections, and right sized her investment in technology at the right time. She gained a 10 percent advantage over the Russell 3000 Growth Index, an amount that contributed to her long-term outperformance for years. Her funds still lost money in the downturn, but her underweight in the tech sector relative to the Russell made an enormous difference. Years later, she still attributes her long-term successful record as a portfolio manager to her actions during this era.

In 2013, Jennifer Uhrig had finally given up her fund to serve on some in-house boards at Fidelity, and I had left almost a decade earlier to cofound Aureus. We see each other often, and once decided to meet at the Twitter IPO lunch being held at the Boston Harbor Hotel. The investment bankers, perhaps to promote an impression of exclusivity, had encased the event in so much security (to weed out the apparent riffraff that always tries to crash investment lunches), that the invitees needed to pass a gauntlet of checkpoints manned by stunning models with commando-type security behind them.

Jennifer had told me she would be there first to save me a seat, and after I maneuvered my way through maximum security, I entered the ballroom where about 150 attendees were sitting down to lunch. As I looked around the room, a waiter asked if I needed some help, and I replied that I was looking for a friend.

The waiter asked what he looked like, and I said my friend was a "she." The waiter responded, "That's easy. There's only one other woman here." He showed me to the table where Jennifer was seated, and I shared the waiter's comment, which was both disturbingly sad and also very funny. We had quite a laugh.

The financial markets test our ability to recognize where risk lies, to say nothing of our capacity to react effectively and sometimes quickly. The market collapse of 2000 offers a perfect case in which undiluted enthusiasm prevailed over measured and logical analysis. Examining reports from that period shows the gross inaccuracies of many of their predictions, but also the blind willingness of investors to accept such forecasts.

We should never discount our own knowledge, training, and skepticism when making investments. Although we might miss out in the near term, when the bubble is inflating, we will generally be rewarded in the long term when reality catches up to dreams.

CHAPTER 10

Risks and Results

Numbers are the tools of my trade. We investment professionals study companies and industries, but we have to prove to ourselves by studying data that the investment we contemplate is attractively priced. We require specific stats, metrics, comps, sequentials, and percentages to provide order and make sense of the market. Even if we know that the price is high, compared with what we might have paid the previous year, we must be able to quantify the reason for the increase.

The numbers are our justification and protection against the risk of losing money. Every day, I watch the prices of stocks flash on my screen in green and red, along with the portfolio weights we carry for each position. Given our obsession with numbers, it is amazing how infrequently we look back through our investing history to study what worked, what did not, and why. I recently reviewed a decade's worth of my firm's historic performance to examine how the tenets of practical risk-taking apply to some of our most notable results—both successful and horrendous.

In this effort, we generated a report that identified the top contributors and detractors to performance over the past decade. There were many holdings for which several principles applied simultaneously, but for others it was clear that we were impacted, sometimes unwittingly, by a benefit or defeat predominantly related to one of the tenets. Analyzing each case offers valuable insight into the application of sensible risk-taking.

GREEN MOUNTAIN COFFEE

Green Mountain Coffee began to take off in early 2010. We noticed its sleek-looking single-serve Keurig coffeemakers and their accompanying colorful pods, a word that I typically associated with peas or small office configurations. Overnight, every high-end financial firm in Manhattan sported a Keurig coffeemaker in its conference room. Despite my embarrassment at being far behind the latest beverage trend, I swallowed my pride and asked how the machine worked. Very easily, I discovered. I don't even drink coffee and I thought it was totally cool.

The producer, Vermont-based Green Mountain Coffee, sold its roasted coffee and beans through retail outlets and mail order. More than a decade earlier, the management had astutely purchased 35 percent of a small Massachusetts company named Keurig, which had patented a single-cup brewing system. By 2006, Green Mountain owned all of Keurig. The combination was a perfect razor–razorblade model—like staples, ink cartridges, or batteries, the disposables generate a profit stream indefinitely while the hardware could be sold at a loss or breakeven.

Upon hearing the management speak at an investor conference, my partners and I set up a time to talk privately with Green Mountain Coffee Roasters (GMCR). We began our process of building our own model for the company, estimating everything from the penetration of the Keurig brewers, the use per machine at homes or in offices, and the proceeds per machine and per pod. In our opinion, Green Mountain could earn $2.00 per share in 2012 or 2013 under a positive scenario. However, the stock had been on a tear since early 2009 and there was the looming risk of future competition.

The patents on single-service K-Cups would begin to expire in 2012 and both Dunkin' Donuts and Starbucks were talking about developing their own single-serving product line. This might throw a sharp curve at Green Mountain's growth trajectory. In addition, the pods were not biodegradable and only part of the container that held the coffee was recyclable. There were rumblings that some municipalities might charge an incremental fee for their waste processing, given the huge number of pods being discarded. The stock in the high thirties was too rich for us; we set a buy target at $30 and hoped we would get our chance.

PROFIT PODS

The opportunity we had been waiting for arrived in September 2010. The SEC announced that it was investigating the company's accounting—never good news for a stock price—and Green Mountain shares tumbled from $36 to $28. We found out what we could about the accounting inquiry and concluded it would likely be years before the case concluded and also that it was improbable the findings would be very severe. We bought the stock. However, because there was still an impending patent cliff and headline risk from the ongoing investigation, we sized our position at about 1.5 percent of our equity holdings, which was approximately half the typical weight. Although it is nearly impossible to calculate the specific risk of one stock purchase relative to another, our analysis suggested that this sizing would preserve our portfolio's overall risk exposure.

Green Mountain resumed its uptrend almost immediately. Instead of competing, both Dunkin' Donuts and Starbucks announced deals with GMCR to create a K-Cup version of their coffee. The earnings advanced ahead of expectations and the stock ticked higher month after month. Not only would Green Mountain earn $2.00 a share, as we anticipated, but over $3.00 was possible for 2013.

The growth in K-Cup sales was astounding. For the year ending September 30, 2009, there were 1.65 billion pods sold, and the estimate for fiscal year 2011, the year we were in, was 4.7 billion—a number that seemed unimaginable for a product with virtually no sales a mere five years earlier. From $30, the shares moved to $60, and kept climbing. We had been buying more stock for new accounts but stopped above $45, because our original target price was in the $55 to $60 range, and a fast 50 percent move forward is often followed by some retracement.

There are more methodologies for valuing companies than there are pages in this book. The market is very wise, and most stocks are priced efficiently. Our goal is to identify those where we think the collective wisdom of all other investors about the value of a share of stock is wrong, where we believe there is substantial upside relative to the price set as equilibrium between buyers and sellers. We use several types of valuation, such as multiples of earnings, cash flow, sum of the parts, and replacement cost. Based on our work, we were comfortable owning Green Mountain Coffee up to the mid-sixties, after which we began to sell it.

By August 2011, when GMCR was in the mid-seventies, we were out of the stock. Across all our accounts, Green Mountain Coffee appreciated over 95 percent and added a full percent to our returns that year. It was truly a great success for us.

After we sold the Green Mountain Coffee stock, it continued to rise, although we thought it was overvalued at that point. So did other investors. Sure enough, in October 2011 a well-known hedge fund manager, David Einhorn, presented a detailed and compelling negative assessment of the stock, suggesting there might be accounting fraud, aggressive sales and earnings projections, and slowing consumption, but also highlighting imminent patent expirations. Investors listened and subsequently drove GMCR stock from $104 all the way to $18 by the middle of 2012. Our sell decision was dangerously close to the torpedo assault, and any larger-sized position might have presented a more complex set of choices about portfolio construction, possibly delaying our action until it was too late.

While I believe that we did right size our Green Mountain weight, we cannot take credit for right timing our sale because we had no idea that Einhorn, the founder and principal investor at Greenlight Capital, was going to speak publicly about the stock or that the effect would be so dramatic. Nevertheless, we did maintain discipline about the extent of our portfolios' exposure to Green Mountain (amusing that its adversary's fund also starts with the same color) and our target price.

Now called Keurig Green Mountain, the company has continued to crank out earnings along with pods of all types. In addition to numerous versions of coffee and tea, there are now cold drink pods, thanks to a joint venture with Coca-Cola, which became a 10 percent owner. The stock not only recovered but surpassed its earlier high, peaking at over $150 in late 2014 before turning down again. We at Aureus have not owned the stock since.

RESEARCH IN MOTION

BlackBerry Limited, the Canadian firm originally called Research in Motion, changed the world of personal communications in the first decade of the millennium. The firm's devices helped establish the smartphone market. The stock's trajectory mirrored its fabulous success in the building of its clientele, and then was crushed by the 2008 market collapse, losing 75 percent of its value. When we began to make purchases in mid-March 2009, we had confidence that high-end smartphones would resume their march toward domination of the mobile communications market. Business and personal spending, we hoped, would creep back as a way of life rather than an indulgence.

BlackBerry survived, and its growth—which had never really slowed—accelerated. The S&P 500 bounced off the bottom and gained

26.5 percent for the year. Our typical stock account gained 40.2 percent in 2009, making it one of our best years. BlackBerry added over 2 percent to our performance, on average, advancing 109 percent for the year in our portfolios. By the end of 2009, most accounts had positions close to 4 percent, making BlackBerry one of our largest weights.

Unfortunately, this is where we should have considered whether such a sizeable investment was appropriate for the level of risk incurred. One of my younger partners, Thad, and I work closely on stock portfolios and rarely argue, but we were having a knockdown fight in the summer of 2010. We could call it a debate or a disagreement, but that would be a lie and a disservice to the caliber of accusations we were throwing at each other. We were not even in the same room. I was vacationing with my family on Cape Cod, or that's what I was supposed to be doing. Instead, I was on the phone with Thad, fighting because BlackBerry had reported a very disappointing quarter and the stock was down 10 percent in after-hours trading.[1] Given that nearly all our accounts had positions of 3 percent or more, such a decline was agonizing.

Ironically, I was driving from Newport, Rhode Island, where one of my sons and I had been visiting the "cottages"—a euphemism for the collection of unbelievably ornate palaces that the industrial barons of the late nineteenth century had built for themselves. We had just completed the "Upstairs, Downstairs" tour of The Breakers, Cornelius Vanderbilt's amazing seventy-room mansion, and now, thanks to the BlackBerry news, I was feeling decidedly "downstairs."

BlackBerry had been a big winner for us. A symbol of the hip and savvy atmosphere of the first decade of the new millennium, the company's smartphone had accumulated twenty-five million subscribers by the end of 2009. Every participant at investor conferences, attendee at fashion shows, and political operative rushing through the halls of Capitol Hill carried a BlackBerry, anxiously scrolling the little centered ball up and down, tapping away on the raised keys, reading, talking—connected. The BlackBerry's encryption technology was considered more "secure" than that of other devices, which was appealing to users who needed to safeguard their own or clients' proprietary information, or who wanted to feel important enough to demand that protection for themselves. To the management, the franchise seemed as secure as its customers' most top-secret e-mails.

iDANGER

The risk to the BlackBerry franchise ultimately arrived in the form of six letters: "iPhone." Apple had released the first version of its well-received, sleek smartphone in 2007, but neither the BlackBerry management nor the supporters on Wall Street considered it a threat because of the BlackBerry's perceived superior security provisions. Despite the continued growth in BlackBerry subscribers—which would top forty million in 2010—and profits, the iPhone tsunami was well on its way to transforming the entire world of personal communications.

In 2009, Apple's installed base surpassed fifty million and was on track to hit one hundred million the following year. Perhaps the encryption technology was inferior, but it was not enough to slow down the insatiable demand for the iPhone. Consumers loved the advanced camera and video features along with the ability to utilize hundreds, and then thousands, of applications—including music, maps, media, and Facebook and other social media sites—which worked seamlessly on Apple's device but awkwardly on the BlackBerry.

So when BlackBerry missed its second-quarter earnings estimate and investors were ditching their shares in the aftermarket, subsequently ruining my vacation day, I sought to make Thad's day a little more frustrating as well.

The earnings miss was now history, and we needed to determine what to do now that the stock was down. We decided to figure out whether the shortfall was an anomaly or a structural change in the phone market. The stock retraced some of its loss, but the management remained obstinate that their product line was fully competitive with

Apple's innovations. Employees began to voice strong preferences for their iPhones, forcing corporate purchasing departments to accept personal choice in devices, which further eroded BlackBerry's client base.

We ended up selling all our BlackBerry stock by the end of September 2010, losing a total of 31 percent for the year on our holding. While that was painful, we made much more money on the name than we lost due to the share price at which we bought it in 2009. While BlackBerry stock has rallied from time to time, the stock trades, in mid-2015, at under $8 per share, compared with a peak of $144 in 2008. Amazingly, there are still forty-six million worldwide subscribers,[2] but that pales compared to the nearly unfathomable five hundred–plus million users of iPhones.[3] Even if this number is high by 50 percent, it's the equivalent of every woman, man, and child in the United States owning an iPhone! BlackBerry never had a chance, and we should have right sized that position earlier.

NET 1 UEPS

Nearly every stock we held in 2008 was a victim of poor timing, but our bet on the South African company Net 1 UEPS was particularly ill fated due to our misjudgment of the timing of the potential upside. From 2005 until 2007, our firm made several successful forays into international holdings, including a Brazilian energy company and a Russian cell phone enterprise. We next decided to research public companies in Africa, where many mineral-rich countries were experiencing strong growth on the back of rising commodity prices. In 2006, we discovered Net 1 UEPS (UEPS), a South African payments- and transactions-processing firm.

The concept was fantastic: as the people of South Africa and neighboring countries prospered, they expected to essentially bypass the brick-and-mortar traditions of the banking industry, with which they had little familiarity anyway, and move directly to initiating transactions via their mobile phones. This included the receipt of wages, pension, welfare, and other payments, which would be powered via Net 1's software platform. The company was already the licensee for state-sponsored benefits payments in several geographies across the country. Net 1 was the odds-on favorite to win many more such licenses, including from the national social security system, or SASSA (South African Social Security Agency).

We met the management of Net 1 UEPS and corresponded over a period of months, building a model that suggested earnings could easily double within five years and the stock price should respond similarly. Were we ever wrong! When the world's financial markets collapsed in 2008, weaker currencies such as the South African rand took a beating, dropping 30 percent. SASSA postponed the awarding of its contracts, which was another major disappointment.

BAD SIGNAL

The essential attraction to Net 1 was timing related: the rapid growth in demand for African commodities, primarily from China; the proliferation of cell phones; the use of these devices for financial transactions; and the probable awarding of benefits software contracts. However, we had the timing wrong. Net 1's mobile phone–based system was several years ahead of both widespread customer demand and a reliable infrastructure on which it would run. The system would require considerably more capital investment before it was fully operational and needed years of test market trials. Earnings of $1.54 per share plummeted to $.06 by 2011 and only returned to the $1.50 level in 2014.[4]

We lost 50 percent on that stock, which we sold in 2009. Although the S&P 500 was recovering in the United States, it was unclear how long it would take foreign markets generally, and the South African market specifically, to catch up. More significantly, the timing of Net 1's rollout plans was being pushed back, probably for years, and we most certainly did not want to wait. Mobile phone–based banking, payroll, and benefits transactions are common in Africa now, but we bet on this transition far too early.

It is often the case that the first mover in a new field—whether it is an Internet search engine such as Yahoo, a browser built by AOL, or a revolutionary social network like MySpace—ends up losing out to better and easier technologies as the innovation pipeline improves. Net 1 was one of the market participants but did not dominate the sector as expected. We made the right move. The stock is still only 25 percent above where we sold it more than six years ago.

FIRST REPUBLIC CORPORATION

With our Net 1 investment we had been burned by a stock from a company with a mission to vitalize the banking experience in Africa, but we had great success with a stock from a company that did participate in the evolution of domestic banking. On this attempt, our timing was right. First Republic (FRC), a San Francisco–based private bank, was one of our best stocks in 2013. We first bought the name in 2011 after a client brought it to our attention because she had met the president of the bank and asked our opinion. We had stayed clear of most financials until that year because of the fallout from the financial crisis, but it was time to move back into the sector as the stocks were selling for prices that discounted continually depressed conditions.

Interestingly, First Republic had gone through several ownership forms. Originally an independent bank, then a public company, and subsequently private, First Republic was then bought by Merrill Lynch, which was forced by its own financial distress to throw itself into the arms of Bank of America. As part of that deal, the U.S. Treasury required Merrill to divest certain assets, including First Republic Bank.

Eventually, the private bank became public again, prompting us to take a close look at the stock in early 2011. There were several compelling aspects to the First Republic story, especially given its focus on the highest end of the market. With the stock market moving upward, individuals were again accumulating wealth. Much of that asset growth was occurring around the Bay Area, with the tremendous explosion of social media enterprises, although the executives at Apple and Google alone could easily populate a private wealth bank.

This ready and willing base of potential clients had a problem; they no longer trusted big banks with their money. Either they had lost a great deal in their accounts at these institutions during the crisis, or they were aghast at the abysmal failure of most of the world's banking giants to manage their own finances.

First Republic represented the antithesis of a stodgy, bloated, controversy-stained bank, and the new money and entrepreneurs of Silicon Valley flocked to it. It also provided excellent service to corporate as well as individual customers. Even as the general economy recovered, the West Coast housing market was rebounding, with FRC a major mortgage originator at the very high end. The timing seemed perfect.

We first purchased the stock in early 2011, but continued to add when the stock dipped over the next year. Our average account return on the position was a gain of 61 percent in 2013, adding close to 2 percent to our overall return that year.[5] Although the company has experienced growing pains, as all public corporations do, the management has executed well on an expansion plan that capitalizes on both changes in the personal wealth management business and the weakness of some of its competitors. We still own the stock.

One of the best and most honest methods to evaluate our skills as stock market investors is to look back at our results and the specific equities that most influence the overall returns. Of course, the effort of squarely confronting our mistakes makes this exercise intimidating. Nevertheless, we can learn from our previous successes and missteps by analyzing how and where we applied the tenets of sensible risk-taking—and where we failed to apply them.

CHAPTER 11

Knowledge and Doubt

It is common sense to gain a deep understanding of a situation before taking on a major risk. In the investment business, information allows us to be more aggressive and offers us protection in defense of our choices.

The relationship between confirming and doubting our personal knowledge is one of the most intriguing in the investment business. The best stocks I have ever bought are ones where we determine something about the company that the market doesn't yet appreciate or value to an appropriate level. The market doesn't value it, that is, until something triggers a revelation that you understood all along—for example, a developer purchases real estate next to the Sahara Casino Resort for a price that makes the casino's worth, and its stock, double.

HARSCO

From Shanghai to Brooklyn, the world was one giant boomtown in 2005, with gleaming towers rising and warehouses being transformed into expensive condominiums. Real estate development was sizzling, and we were playing that move in our portfolios with a public U.S. realty brokerage company and a French cement maker, but we started to look for a more direct move into construction.

Harsco Corporation, formerly Harrisburg Car Manufacturing Company, originally served the railroad industry in the mid-nineteenth century, fashioning railcars, track, and peripheral services for steel and railroad companies in Western Pennsylvania and Ohio. Over time, Harsco turned its engineering skills to, among other things, construction-related product lines, including scaffolding, forming, and shoring from industrial real estate it created, to platforms on which to move these skeletal structures. Not only were Harsco's movable construction apparatus in strong rental demand in the U.S. and Europe, but the growth in emerging markets, particularly in Asia and the Middle East, during the early years of the millennium provided Harsco with multiple new clients and projects.

We studied the different divisions of Harsco and decided that the key to the story was the "access services" segment, which accounted for roughly 30 percent of the $3 billion in 2005 revenue. In our opinion, if the demand for platforms and highly engineered scaffolding and other services continued to grow at a prolific rate over the next few years, Harsco would enjoy both full utilization of its construction equipment but also the ability to raise its rental rates to developers, whether these were private groups, municipalities, or countries.

After positive impressions during our first phase of research, we arranged a meeting with Gene Truett, Harsco's treasurer, and with the company's charismatic CEO, Derek Hathaway, a Scot who quit school to help support his family at age fifteen and built a company in Europe that Harsco acquired. Hathaway was also adept at charming his U.S. investors with his thick brogue. The Middle East contributed less than 10 percent of revenues in 2005, and Asia even less. However, there were substantial new orders from government-backed projects in the United Arab Emirates (UAE), specifically Dubai and Abu Dhabi, involving the construction of numerous towers, including the world's tallest building, the Burj Dubai, now known as the Burj Khalifa.

My partners and I modeled the sales and earnings potential for each of the Harsco divisions. We felt confident enough about our own projections to buy the stock across our portfolios in the fourth quarter of 2005.

The purchase was a winner. In 2006, the return on Harsco positions, which exceeded a 4 percent weight for our accounts, was over 70 percent. Revenue and earnings growth exceeded Wall Street's estimates, mostly due to the access services division, as we had expected. However, by the end of 2006, we were considering how much heat was left in the real estate market.

I was going to Kuwait to review a portfolio with a client, so I arranged a detour to the UAE to tour Harsco's projects there with the Middle East director to get a better sense of the scope and potential of that operation. After a couple of days in Kuwait, where I imagined, on several occasions, that I might test out the theory about frying an egg on pavement, I flew to the city-state of Dubai.

My morning began inauspiciously when I reached the lobby of the Jumeirah Hotel and realized that people were staring at me because my short-sleeved top was insufficiently discreet. Despite the expected 106-degree temperature, all the women in Western dress were wearing suits and most others were wearing traditional floor-length black abayas. I rushed back upstairs to grab a jacket, feeling horribly misled by images I recalled from television commercials of a socially liberal culture with smiling couples in skimpy beachwear. Obviously, they were not filming in my hotel lobby.

Henrik,* the Harsco regional president, found me in the busy lobby. He was a tall German with long hair who fulfilled my impression that the city was full of Wild West–type prospectors. After a decade with the company's European construction group, he had accepted the

---

* Henrik is a pseudonym.

promotion to run the Emirates division, which Henrik expected to cata-
pult his career. We drove to the local headquarters, passing one major
building project after another, where I met with the other members of
the broadly international team, all of whom had vast experience in commercial construction across multiple continents.

They answered my questions about conducting business in the Middle East compared to other geographies, such as the challenges from
lack of water and the heat, and the advantage of cheap energy. Henrik,
the chief engineer, and I then drove to a nearby airfield and boarded a
helicopter. We flew over all of Dubai and then to Abu Dhabi and Shar-
jah, another of the states of the United Arab Emirates. Most striking
was the sheer number of cranes and construction sites. One long artery
in Dubai appeared to be re-creating the height and internal square foot-
age of about twenty blocks of Park Avenue at once, as skeletons of one
skyscraper after another rose from the desert. Just as amazing were the
newly created star-shaped islands emerging from the gulf, on which
thousands of luxury homes were being built. We flew above partially
completed luxury hotels, sports arenas, and shopping centers, all glis-
tening steel and glass in the blazing sun. If I had not seen it that day, I
doubt I would have believed it.

We circled the tallest structure in the world, which in 2006 was
four years from completion, but already incredibly impressive. The Burj
Dubai, later renamed Burj Khalifa for Sheikh Khalifa, the emir of Abu
Dhabi and president of the UAE, stands 2,717 feet, with 163 floors. It
represents the pinnacle of Dubai's strategy to join the world's greatest
centers of commerce and become a magnet for the global jet set, providing space where they could play, shop, and reside. The Harsco executives were intimately involved in several aspects of the Burj construction,
and they described to me the way the developer used their equipment. I
asked if we could go onsite but the response was a firm negative.

Henrik told me that the city of Dubai had borrowed $80 billion
from the government and ruling families of the United Arab Emirates to fund this huge statewide development. While the population of

Dubai is close to two million, more than 70 percent are expatriates from Asia who mostly serve as laborers. I began to wonder who would live in all these expensive condominiums, own the houses on the man-made islands, and work in all these millions of square feet of office space. Maybe this story, while phenomenally impressive, was actually more fantasy than reality.

If Harsco's clients in the Middle East began to feel pinched financially, they might renege on their contract commitments, leaving the company without rent on costly equipment. There were projects from Dubai to Jakarta powered by easy debt, and Harsco was very leveraged to this phenomenon. This felt like a bubble that would soon pop. My enthusiasm was quickly turning to skepticism.

When I returned to Boston, my partners and I reviewed the pros and cons and concluded that we should begin to sell the stock. The stock market and Harsco's management were just too optimistic about future profits, in our opinion. Then, of course, the 2008 "sandstorm" hit the fan. Dozens of half-completed giant structures along Dubai's central boulevard were abandoned. Harsco suffered severe financial loss—in part because all its product lines were hit by the great recession, but also because the corporation had added facilities, people, and debt, and invested extensively right at the top. As of 2015, the firm has yet to fully recover.

We made money on our Harsco stock because we learned as much as we could about its business lines, clients, growth opportunities, and the potential risks. We understood that the party, not quite in full swing when we initially invested, was soon going to end, and the aftermath would be ugly.

ALLIED IRISH BANK

By mid-2007, we were nervous about U.S. financial institutions. My partner, David Scudder, was sufficiently convinced that banks and other loan providers were abusing the subprime mortgage market and suggested that we sell most of our holdings in that sector. Since we were "naked," or unexposed to financials entirely, we began to look outside the United States for a company about which we would feel more comfortable.

We zeroed in on Allied Irish Bank (AIB) after studying a number of international banks. The Irish economy had been growing its GDP at a rapid annual clip of 4.5 to 5.7 percent since 2004, and prospects remained very strong according to the management of the bank, economists, and our contacts in Great Britain.

In our eagerness to add a financial name to our portfolio, we ignored what I had realized on my trip to Dubai; that investors had been pouring billions and billions into real estate projects that might ultimately go bust. I get nauseous when I now think about how we disregarded such signs of risk. Unfortunately, we listened to people who were in denial that a similar bubble was percolating in their own country.

We spoke with a good friend of mine who lived in Dublin and worked at Allied Irish Bank, and she confirmed that the Irish housing and real estate market was in much better shape than that of the United States. The stock was selling for a modest price/earnings multiple of eight times last twelve months' earnings per share. We read extensively about the company, built our own earnings model, felt good about our numbers, and bought the stock in September of 2007.

Within weeks, we knew that we had made a mistake. In March of 2008, just as the temperature of the housing market was beginning to boil, AIB asserted that 8 percent of its housing portfolio might have some credit quality problems. "Might" was a euphemism for "did," and 8 percent seemed like an optimistic number given the large proportion of the loan portfolio connected to housing and commercial property. A Deutsche Bank analyst wrote in March 2008, "As far as credit quality for AIB is concerned, however, the forward looking indications remain good."[1] Nicely stated but horribly wrong.

We had worked on understanding the domestic mortgage climate, concluding that it was dangerous. I saw the same with the real estate market in the Middle East, and understood that the bad loan virus had been spreading around the world. However, we blindly ignored what we knew and made a bad investment in a country that we failed to study sufficiently. Shortly thereafter, the property market in Ireland collapsed, and the bank acknowledged its exposure to bad property loans and overextended developers.

The value of homes and commercial buildings supporting Allied's loans was overstated. As soon as we suspected trouble, in January 2008, we sold our entire position, taking a 12 percent loss, which was tough, but a consolation given that the stock essentially became worthless just two years later. Allied Irish Bank accepted a bailout from the Irish government to stay afloat, reported losses from 2009 until 2013, and only returned to profitability in 2014. We should have known better.

DOUBT

With the glut of information available in the investment industry, the ability to apply healthy skepticism is, as I have shown, a key factor in sensible risk-taking. Doubting what other investors tell us they know is as valuable as having a deep understanding of the subject in question, particularly when we can prove that we are right.

For most of the 1990s, Gap Inc. was an incredible growth story and an amazingly impressive stock, rising tenfold between 1995 and 1999. The company defined casual but stylish apparel, revolutionizing the retail industry with innovations that included stacking inventory rather than hanging it all on racks. The merchandise was comfortable and somewhat unisex, and the ad campaigns were catchy.

However, I recall a meeting in 1998 in which CEO Mickey Drexler, who is often credited with the brand's meteoric rise, commented that Gap accounted for slightly over 3 percent, or $6.5 billion, of total U.S. retail clothing sales and that this number could easily rise to the mid to high single digits. This claim seemed grandiose and rather implausible to me, considering the wildly fickle and short-lived nature of fashion trends. Not only do consumer tastes change, but new competitors emerge, such as J.Crew and H&M, both of which learned from Gap's earlier success. That was the day I lost confidence in Gap. It also happened to coincide with the peak of Gap's penetration of the U.S. clothing industry and of its stock price.

TWITTER

As I described earlier, I attended the initial public offering roadshow for Twitter. The Boston Harbor Hotel lobby, hallways, and ballroom were full of young, lean, unclosely shaven men wearing expensive, European-cut tapered shirts and no ties. The assembled men seemed to follow the same style guidebook: *How to Look Like a Tech Entrepreneur or Digital Age Investor.*

I would not go so far as to say that arrogance is an occupational hazard in my business, but I almost just did. If you are an executive promoting your company to potential investors, you need to be as positive and self-confident as possible because your aim is to convince your audience to purchase your stock. If you are a fund manager, you need to have confidence in your portfolio choices, in tough as well as strong markets, and one of the best ways to boost your stocks is to persuade peers in the business that they should buy your stock right now.

I was interested in learning why Twitter should be valued close to $20 billion. As a platform, Twitter primarily engages users as they follow, share, and respond to the musings and postings of often famous or notable people. Advertisers target high-profile users' posts and the consumers who gravitate toward certain categories—so Kim Kardashian's followers may see ads for Las Vegas nightclubs, mascara, and Manolo Blahnik shoes.

Even with my vast exposure to self-promotion, I would place the Twitter management presentation that day at the top of my hype-quotient bar graph. We heard that Twitter's goal was to be used by "everyone on the planet!" The statement was so bold and encompassing that I spent the next minute or so wondering whether animals were included in "everyone," and if Twitter would move on to Venus after conquering Earth.

We decided to pass on this deal. I was skeptical of the revenue and profit projections for Twitter, despite the 232 million worldwide monthly active users (MAU) the platform had already retained. More than 75 percent of regular Twitter users were overseas, and advertising models beyond the U.S. and Western Europe were much less developed.[2] At the expected company valuation, there was no room for disappointment.

On the first day of trading, in early November of 2013, the stock opened at $26 and later closed at $44.93 before rocketing to $73 by the end of the year. That was the peak; since then, Twitter stock has sunk below $30 and CEO Dick Costolo resigned over such discouraging results.

In order to evaluate where the company failed to meet forecasts, I read several Wall Street analyst reports—including one from J. P. Morgan—that estimated revenues would more than double by 2015. The J. P. Morgan report went on to forecast that Twitter would have 366 million average monthly users by 2015.[3]

In reality, most of the metrics have actually exceeded expectations. Unfortunately, the growth in users has stalled and even turned negative domestically. Monthly average users, predicted to be 366 million, are currently estimated at 335 million for 2015. When companies have lofty expectations built into their stock prices, the market has no tolerance for shortfalls.

While it is unclear whether Twitter users have grown permanently tired of the unrelenting parade of tweets, or if some retooling of the platform will reinvigorate user growth, the platform has lost its allure to investors, who have fled to the "safety" of the more established Facebook and Amazon. We have been skeptical from day one and have still not bought the stock.

When we buy a stock, it is because we believe that the market does not yet fully appreciate the full potential of the company. Often, we are simply not skeptical enough. Without qualification, I can say that I have believed at various (and wrong) times that Motorola would compete effectively in the smartphone market; radio-advertising rates would climb; three-dimensional imaging would become the norm for most X-rays; the Canadian apparel business would consolidate and improve; and speech recognition would take a large share of typed communication.

KYTHERA

Lack of skepticism is deadly but the history of the stock market suggests that a positive bias is valuable, since the market has increased over time, and excess cynicism can easily paralyze you into inaction. The winning strategy is often to question the extreme negative market sentiment about a company, which is exactly what we did with Kythera Biopharmaceuticals.

In early 2013, shortly after we had sold BioMarin, a biotech stock, at a nice profit, we began to comb for an attractive replacement in the sector, which maintained positive momentum. A dermatologist friend suggested that I do some work on Kythera, a recently public Southern California biotechnology corporation whose lead product was a remedy for double chins. We read through all the clinical studies on the primary compound, ATX-101, an injected acid-based drug that miraculously disrupted the membranes of fat cells, which were then naturally cleared from the system. The Phase 2 data, released in 2011, showed strong efficacy in eliminating the submental fat—double chins, in layman's terms.

Kythera was now running Phase 3 studies with more than five hundred participants, which would hopefully generate strong enough results to garner the FDA approval needed for commercial production.

The stock was selling in the high twenties, yet there was very little enthusiasm on Wall Street for Kythera. Analysts considered a treatment for double chins to be nothing short of a joke, and the firm's market value, at under $800 million, reflected such investor indifference.

Having owned Allergan, the producer of Botox—the billion-dollar antiwrinkle drug—I was a solid proponent of aesthetic dermatology products, perhaps because I could easily envision how I might benefit. This was a proven growing business sector in which patients paid in full, and everyone from aging baby boomers to thirty-five-year-old film stars of both genders employed the products in hopes of besting Father Time.

I visited Kythera at its headquarters an hour outside of Los Angeles to meet the management team. About half the staff, including CEO Keith Leonard and CFO John Smither, appeared to have arrived from Amgen, with the other half coming from Allergan, the two large biopharmaceutical corporations in the area. I wanted to fully understand the clinical design of the Phase 3 studies, which, in my opinion, is where firms fail to correctly address key factors such as the number of patients, the definitions of success, the dosing regimen, length of the trial, and multiple other elements that might impact the results. I had a long list of questions, not all of which the management was willing to answer, but I was impressed with the team's careful research and thorough responses to many of my inquiries.

We modeled out the potential for ATX-101, making conservative assumptions about the percentage of Americans with double chins who would seek the drug, the cost per treatment, its profitability, and the sales and marketing expenses, and we arrived at an earnings per share in 2018 of over $5.00. It was our belief that if we could purchase the stock below $30 it had tremendous upside.

After our internal meeting, we made a relatively small initial purchase of Kythera at around $29 per share. When the very positive Phase 3 clinical trial results were announced in September 2013, the stock spiked but later fell back to our cost level in 2014. The market was skeptical about whether the FDA would approve a drug that offered less a health benefit and more an emotional uplift, but we bought on every dip. Kythera's management visited our office in Boston on more than one occasion, and I continued to see the company whenever I was in Los Angeles.

The FDA approved ATX-101, brand name Kybella, on April 29, 2015. Despite that success, in early May Kythera shares were trading only in the low forties, where we acquired it in new accounts. I needed to travel West in mid-June and had set up a meeting with the company to review the new drug launch and the program for developing the next product, a novel therapy for baldness.

When my plane landed at LAX, the first message I saw was from the investor relations' director at Kythera, cancelling my appointment for the following day, June 16, without explanation. Having just flown three thousand miles, I stared at my phone in disbelief, anger, and frustration. The company spokesperson, whom I knew fairly well, was apologetic, but also very clear that no senior executives from Kythera were available. I asked whether the CEO had a serious health problem, and she said no; I tried a couple of other probing questions but got nowhere, and then we signed off.

The stock price had been rising steadily for a few weeks, and I would have bet the reason that executives would not see me was because Kythera was being acquired. I called my office. Even though I had no specific information, I knew it would be unwise for us to buy any shares. The last thing we needed was a call from the SEC asking why we had been buying stock in a corporation right before it sold out, if that was indeed the outcome. Most of Aureus's accounts already held positions of over 2 percent.

Sure enough, the first story I saw on my phone, on my iPad, and on CNBC when I woke in Los Angeles on June 17 was that Allergan—the large biopharma company from which many of Kythera's staff had migrated—had announced that it was purchasing the smaller firm for $2.1 billion, or $75 per share. My initial reaction was, *Wow*. It's always a great feeling to be vindicated on an investment that the market had ignored for years. Kythera stock had traded as low as $42 merely six weeks before the buyout, showing that our skepticism of the market's own cynicism was one of the best applications of sensible risk-taking we had made in years.

MetroPCS

The record of every professional investor, whether or not she admits it, is littered with "sucker!" episodes of misplaced faith. We love to believe in the amazing medical cure and the one-of-a kind retail product that everyone wants and needs, as well as the technology that will encounter no competition for a decade. Although the human bias is generally positive, skepticism, as a tenet to risk-taking, assures some balance. Despite my heavily cynical leanings when I first encounter a new company, I have fallen for my share of "great" ideas.

In 2007 we heard the MetroPCS Communications pitch from the CEO of a major venture capital firm that had invested in several early rounds of financing. Their analysis suggested that a sizable minority of the population would prefer to purchase cell phone minutes in a prepaid plan within a local region, controlling the cost, rather than allowing their phone bill to balloon with overage charges. We spoke to MetroPCS several times and visited a number of store locations to talk to the managers as well as to monitor traffic. After our visits we believed that we understood the platform, the geographic growth strategy, and a realistic model of PCS's revenues and costs over the next few years.

The company and its supporters were woefully off base. MetroPCS (PCS) had not anticipated that rival carriers would offer increasingly attractive plans with unlimited geographic reach within the United States. The marginal cost of minutes kept falling, and customers ended up sticking with their legacy plans. Its phones were not as advanced as what the public, even those with the least generous plans, demanded. Meanwhile, MetroPCS spent wildly on expansion, advertising, and promotional marketing, which both decimated its profitability and disappointed shareholders immensely. The stock lost 50 percent of its value in 2007, and our only consolation was that it was never a large enough position to do much damage to our performance.

It is clear that we benefit as investors, as well as decision makers and risk takers, when we take the time to gain a deep understanding of the prospective investment. Knowledge is an invaluable resource that we should apply before diving into risk-related pursuits, and with investing there is publicly available information that anyone can employ in his own analysis. As we review our past returns, we become better at appreciating risk and taking sensible actions that incorporate the tenets.

CHAPTER 12

Masters of the Trade

Over my career, I have had the honor and the privilege of working with some incredible investors. In my discussions with them, these investors rarely addressed risk specifically, but it is clear that they innately apply the tenets of practical risk-taking to their stock decisions.

They are naturally skeptical of projections and forecasts until they have spent time with the reports and developed a deep understanding of each investment allocation. The sharpest professional investors have a razor-like focus on the key factors that will move a stock up or down, and they do not lose sight of these variables despite market gyrations. While their styles vary, there is an obvious consistency among these investors with regard to attention to detail, sizing of their bets, the price they pay, and the timing of their purchases and sales.

ROOM KEYS, CHIPS, AND VAULTS

When I joined Fidelity after business school, in the summer of 1983, Peter Lynch was already a star. Magellan was one of the clear top performers among large U.S. stock mutual funds, and over the course of the next seven years my peers and I in the research department showered Peter with attention and only our best ideas. We climbed over one another for face time and desperately tried to impress him with our dedication, our prodigious research productivity, and, most of all, our well-timed stock recommendations. Peter was always polite, sometimes distracted, soft spoken, opinionated in an articulate way, and, in the old days, enamored of the mountains of paper that grew from all ledges and the perimeter carpeting in his office. Physically, he is tall and square jawed, with a wild mane of hair that morphed from salt and pepper to white over the years, standing at various angles from his scalp à la Andy Warhol.

On the Monday morning following the Sunday evening that I delivered my first set of twins, in 1983, I called Peter at 7 a.m., knowing that he would be in the office. When I reported our news, he enthused, "Great, great, great, great…" many times, as he often did after hearing something positive or potentially exciting. After a brief pause he inquired if I had spoken with the management of Security Pacific, a West Coast bank I had visited about a month earlier, and whose stock we had been buying. I expected his question, and after I informed him of my conversation with the bank he uttered a few more "greats."

Over the years, I spent a lot of time with Peter as an assistant fund manager on Magellan, an industry analyst, and a sector fund manager before he retired from running the fund in May of 1990. He still works at Fidelity as an advisor and mentor, and holds "legend" status among the employees whose careers he helped launch and those who were not yet born or were still in diapers when his Magellan tenure ended.

Speaking with Peter about the framework of his risk analysis yielded unique insights into his style of investing. Instead of using a specific methodology, he grounded his analysis in an intuition that pervaded his assessments. During his thirteen-year tenure, the annualized return on Magellan Fund was 29.2 percent. This was nearly double the strong return of the S&P 500. An investment of $1,000 in the fund on May 31, 1977, would have been worth $27,000 on May 31, 1990![1] Whether or not Peter and I use the same vocabulary about risk, he clearly maintained an innate ability to size, time, understand, and apply appropriate skepticism to stock trading.

One of Peter's largest bets in my early years at Fidelity was La Quinta Motor Inns. Peter liked the lodging sector, as Americans were traveling much more frequently for business in the 1980s, which was reflected in the constant addition of new airline routes. He owned a couple of public lodging companies whose managements praised one of their competitors, La Quinta Motor Inns. Peter was so impressed by these accolades that he contacted La Quinta immediately.

La Quinta, originally a Texan motel chain, had a unique business model that revolutionized the industry: the facilities were deliberately located very close to restaurants, eliminating the costly dining operation, function rooms, elaborate kitchens, and splashy lobbies. By adopting this strategy, the company could provide larger rooms for rates 20 percent below those of traditional hotel chains. Because the headquarters was in Texas, few money managers had noticed La Quinta, so the stock was very reasonably priced given the earnings and the growth prospects. Peter bought up a huge position in the company, which generated nearly ten times its cost during his holding period.

Peter knew that the business travel market was at the tip of a very long runway—a growing number of road warriors needed clean, reasonably priced lodging. The timing was right for a new lodging entrant, and La Quinta was well positioned to capitalize on this expanding market. This was the type of stock on which Peter Lynch built his track record. He owned a large enough position to make a significant difference to Magellan's returns.

I began studying the gaming industry soon after I started at Fidelity. Peter was convinced by the half-mile-long lines outside the new

Atlantic City casinos that Americans loved to gamble, and he wanted to participate in that growing market. Resorts International, the first East Coast gaming facility, had opened in 1978, and visitors from New York and Philadelphia were flocking there in droves. But the real action, Peter knew, would be in Las Vegas.

Despite the city's balmy climate and endless spatial capacity, which its Northeastern counterpart clearly lacked, Las Vegas had been in a slump for a decade. A series of high-profile mob-related scandals and arrests had cast a dark shadow over the city. By the early 1980s, however, a new gaming commission, much tighter regulations, and greater FBI scrutiny of the industry had cleaned up the players and encouraged more mainstream participants to enter the market. The fact that the mutual fund community in Boston and New York was still reluctant to embrace an industry so recently associated with organized crime was one of the reasons stocks such as Caesars, Golden Nugget (the brainchild of Steve Wynn, which was renamed Mirage a few years later), Circus Circus, and Sahara were so attractively priced.

After a few trips to Atlantic City, I headed west to Las Vegas, Nevada. The city was entering a more corporate, albeit glitzy, phase, and as I approached the Sahara, the enormous and brightly lit marquee inviting guests to their gaming tables read, "Welcome Kari Firestone from Fidelity Investments." I suppressed my urge to direct the cab driver to turn around and find me another place to stay.

Despite my hesitation, I spent hours with then-CEO of the Sahara, Paul Lowden, reviewing the company's shaky finances and determining its eligibility for a loan to finance a new tower, remodel the casino floor, revitalize some land for an amusement park, and refinance its high-interest debt. Although the sheer number of pieces that needed to fall into place seemed overwhelming, the state, the city, and the financial institutions in Las Vegas were eager to support any novel projects following years of stagnation. If Lowden could pull off his plans, a stock price of $3 was an incredible bargain. I met with some bankers in town, built an earnings model, and felt confident in my recommendation to Peter that we purchase a large position in Sahara. Even if the casino never made money, the value of its property, ideally located at the end of the Las Vegas Strip, would rise dramatically as development moved in Sahara's direction.

Las Vegas was on the verge of a renaissance; the time was right. In 1984, the city had yet to begin construction on the numerous casino-hotels that dominate the current skyline. Between 1989 and 1999, the industry leaders opened Mirage, Excalibur, Treasure Island, Monte Carlo, Bellagio, the Venetian, and the Paris casinos, each its own vast enterprise. The main thoroughfare of the city is now so densely developed that it is nearly impossible to imagine that during my two-mile runs from Caesars Palace to the Sahara and back, tumbleweeds would often roll across my path from the desert-like vacant lots on either side of the Strip.

We bought enough casino stocks to influence the returns for Magellan and other funds whose managers believed in the gaming industry. However, we lacked the sophisticated tools of modern risk management, instead owning whatever percentage of a company, such as 5 percent or 10 percent, was allowable internally. Today, stock investors, professionals, and laymen alike can learn with a keystroke the weight, to the second decimal point, of their holdings, the relative positioning, and expected volatility versus their benchmarks. These tools were not as easily available in the 1980s when Peter Lynch ran Magellan Fund. Although fund managers thirty years ago might not have studied a report detailing their "active bets" relative to a benchmark, we had enough information to know where we were placing our money. If Magellan held gaming companies with a combined weight exceeding 6 percent, Peter Lynch knew he was wagering on the success of the sector.

Peter held a deep knowledge of the companies in which he was investing, both through his own intuition and via analysts like me. I traveled to Atlantic City and Las Vegas so frequently that it was a joke among our friends. When people asked where I was, David would exclaim, "Oh, back in Vegas."

I knew the profitability of all the table games and slots by casino, spent one evening watching a Chinese national lose more than a million dollars playing baccarat, discussed the pros and cons of the game from the house's viewpoint with an off-duty pit boss, and watched with the head of security at Bally's from one-way glass above the casino floor as he tracked a team of card counters.

Peter Lynch looked for industries on the brink of explosive growth or in turmoil. During the S&L crisis from the mid-1980s to the mid-1990s, over a third of the industry was shut down by regulators or filed for bankruptcy. Regardless, according to Peter, the savings and loan stocks were the "best" industry overweight he ever made. Banks in numerous states—with Texas as a key example—collapsed under the weight of their own excess borrowing, bad loans, and weak adherence to industry guidelines. Regulators, under pressure from Congress, applied strict new standards for their local institutions, all of which were limited within single states, and the shares of surviving savings and loan entities took a tremendous hit.

Peter and a small team pored over seemingly endless balance sheets from hundreds of banks, obsessing over even the smallest details. To determine where the regulators may have been too lenient or too punitive on loans, my colleagues questioned the executives of these institutions, learning as many details as possible. To comply fully with regulators, many savings and loans took significant hits to earnings as they increased their bad loan reserve. The West Newton Savings Bank, a suburban S&L in Newton, Massachusetts, under pressure from regulators, wrote down its loan portfolio to pennies on the dollar.

In the impending slaughter that eviscerated the share value of nearly all its peers, the stock price cratered over 75 percent. Peter anticipated that the bank would eventually recover a much higher percentage of the value of its loans. Magellan acquired a large stake in the company, well below $4 per share. When Fleet National Bank bought West Newton Savings in 1994 the price reached $25.

Bank boards, executives, and other investors were shell shocked and skeptical, but Peter Lynch saw the potential worth of these institutions and bought the stocks of many dozens of banks and S&Ls during the late 1980s, making a huge profit on them. He, like all great investors, has a natural ability to right time an opportunity, seizing on it well before the general market accepts the positive attributes that he perceives as inevitable. Peter knew instinctively what weight would impact his fund and generally recognized when a sector was undergoing a hugely positive transformation that would blow these stocks skyward. The transformation could follow a disaster such as the S&L crisis; it could be the cleanup, rebuilding, and accessibility of Las Vegas to a national customer base; or it could be the emergence of Americans' insatiable appetite for cable television. Peter and our analysts knew these companies and industries cold, but he never failed to challenge every number that looked suspiciously optimistic or did not make absolute sense.

I remember hearing George Vanderheiden, an immensely skilled investor who had spent years as a technology analyst, talk about Intel at a group meeting in my early months at Fidelity. He was soft spoken, earnest, and professorial looking. George never speaks unless he is totally clear on the specific topic, and that was obvious to me in 1983.

I owe a major advance in my career to George—in 1998 he chose me to succeed him as the manager of Destiny Fund. George tends to talk mainly about overall market strategy, sentiment, and technical factors yet his underlying approach to stock selection incorporates the same sensible risk-taking I have observed in other talented fund managers.

TRENDS AND TRAJECTORY

When George Vanderheiden took the reins of Destiny Fund in 1980, his first major decision was to ensure the right sizing of his new fund's energy sector weight. The previous manager had seriously underweighted energy stocks during a very strong period when oil and gas stocks outperformed all other industry groups, causing underperformance for more than a year. George believed these stocks were expensive and refused to increase the weight of the industry group. This analysis proved correct, and the oil and gas stocks peaked a month later, which helped Destiny's performance significantly.

George made some large bets in his fund on technology stocks, many of which he had followed as a research analyst. Over time, he began to appreciate that breakthroughs often sprang from the equipment manufacturing companies that served the semiconductor industry. These enterprises—Applied Materials, Lam Research, Novellus Systems, and KLA Instruments—were highly innovative and responsible for the exponential expansion in chip computing power. He bought each of these stocks, which later proved among the largest contributors to his fund's performance for more than a decade.

However, George changed his opinion of technology stocks in the late 1990s during the heady tech bubble. George always thinks about the big picture, considering valuation, sentiment, and fundamentals. His key philosophy is to avoid those groups that are overvalued and over-loved, and that offer no room for disappointment. This perfectly defined the situation with the technology industry at the end of the millennium. In other words, George chose to underweight, or right size, this entire market sector, which, like energy in 1980, was overvalued.

As a former semiconductor analyst, George understood the technology sector and its terminology but he could not embrace the market's obsession with dot-com stocks, which he thought were severely overvalued. He was highly skeptical of the companies' own guidance, and thought that Wall Street estimates in 1999 were totally unrealistic. The Federal Reserve was raising rates, and this could slow the overheated economy. The market seemed dangerously high, and he positioned the $30 billion he managed in the Growth Opportunities Fund very conservatively.

Every day in late 1999 and early 2000, as the market climbed into bubble-bursting territory, George questioned his resolve, but he never wavered. He knew from previous experience that if you intend to sell positions in a large fund, you need to be early. If you wait too long and the market starts to unravel, you simply cannot unload them without being caught in an avalanche. Also, the sheer number of shares that Fidelity funds own can push stocks up or down, further exacerbating the prevailing price action. When the Nasdaq peaked in January 2000, George's largest positions included such old economy stocks as U.S. Trust and Philip Morris.

George was correct in his defensive portfolio positioning in 1999, but he told me to always keep in mind a very important concept: the trend is your friend. In market terms, this means that moves in either direction can persist much longer than an informed investor thinks logical. Sentiment, which is obviously psychological rather than quantitative, has a very real impact on markets and should not be ignored. George admits to, at times, placing less weight on sentiment than would be optimal. This could relate to consumer demand for Beanie Babies, syndication rights to the *Cosby Show*, or the value of a drug to treat a worldwide patient population of one thousand.

Markets get carried away, buyers overpay, and then years later, after all the write-offs, bankruptcies, and tears, everyone looks back and acts as though, of course, the right course was obvious. I think that George is too hard on himself. It's impossible to time the peak perfectly, and his long-term track record illustrates that he has been very good at recognizing overvaluation.

George protected his shareholders on the downside in 2000 much better than most mutual fund managers did, including me. Every accomplished investor I interviewed over the age of fifty described the Internet stock mania and the subsequent collapse as one of the most traumatic periods of his career. This was true whether that experience turned out to be a career success or failure. My greatest regret as a fund manager is that I did not follow George's example and avoid the damage from the bursting tech bubble. Unlike George, I was not cynical enough.

MEDIA MAESTRO

When I started to follow media and entertainment stocks in the 1980s, the name Gordon Crawford was already being invoked by the management of companies and Wall Street analysts, who cited Crawford's investment as an inducement to buy the stock. Very quietly, they would whisper, "You know, Gordy at Capital [Capital Group in Los Angeles] owns a *huge* position."

Gordon Crawford started at Capital Group in 1971 and had the good luck to cover the sector most identified with Los Angeles. If knowledge is one of the key elements of sensible risk-taking, knowing the principals who start, build, and lead the companies in an industry is enormously helpful to one's understanding of and insights into that sector. During my years following and investing in the biotechnology industry, I had the luxury of building relationships with luminaries in the field at Harvard and MIT. When they cofounded new firms or joined a scientific advisory board, I could ask them about the science behind the concept and about their collaborators. As the entertainment analyst at the only mutual fund complex located in the film production center of the world, Gordy had the same type of access and advantage.

Capital Group operates under a model in which the analysts invest a portion of each fund in their area of coverage. In contrast, the decision making at Fidelity's diversified funds was controlled by the fund's sole portfolio manager, albeit with ample help from industry analysts who offer their stock recommendations. Crawford saw his role as finding well-priced, exciting companies in which Capital could take large positions, often more than 10 percent, and spread this investment across several of Capital's growth-oriented funds.

Similar to other investors with whom I spoke, Gordy did not think specifically about the size of the risk but more about determining, through intense research, the upside potential of the company. Once he identified a great opportunity, he and his associates would often make that stock a 3 to 5 percent weight in a single fund.

Most Americans do not remember the days before cable, when we had only three commercial networks and public broadcasting, but cable television was a brand-new service in the 1970s. Gordy became an expert on the economics of the business. He noted that many investors complained shortsightedly about the lack of cable company profitability, but they were ignoring the basic format of the nascent industry. After winning the bid to provide cable television to a new municipality, the operator needed to spend heavily to build out the entire area-wide cable plant, then market heavily to attract subscribers. Therefore, the company operated in the red for the first few years in a new territory, until penetration began to ramp up and the system became highly profitable. By that time, the operator was constructing a new system that again dragged down net income. Eventually, Gordy knew, all the cable systems would be in the black.

In addition, the federal government handed the cable industry a huge win in 1984, which cemented its potential upside for years to come. The Cable Communications Policy Act of 1984 effectively allowed cable television operators monopoly status and pricing freedom within each distinct geographic region, accepting the industry argument that no company would undertake the huge cost of construction if a second firm was granted the rights to enter the market with a competing system. I began to follow the stocks in 1986, when they were in a perfect phase of expansion and value creation. Peter Lynch's Magellan and many other Fidelity funds, along with Gordon Crawford, were heavy owners of the stocks.

Gordy also knew that that the entire landscape of entertainment delivery and consumption was being radically transformed. At the same time that he was gobbling up 10 percent or more of Comcast, Tele-Communications, Inc. (TCI), Daniels, Charter, and Cablevision, he led Capital Group funds into large positions in the content suppliers who would provide programming to fill the numerous new channels, such as Warner Communications (soon to merge with Time Inc.), the Walt Disney Company, and MCA Universal.

TCI, the largest of the cable operators, also owned minority interests in many programming entities. John Malone, TCI's CEO, decided to split the company before incurring any antitrust problems with the government. He structured the deal so that TCI shareholders were issued rights they could exchange, with additional cash, for shares in the new company. Liberty Media would hold fourteen cable systems plus interest in many cable channels and other programming suppliers. These included portions of the Black Entertainment Network (BET), American Movie Classics (AMC), Turner Broadcasting, Home Shopping Network, and the majority of QVC, the other large cable-shopping network.

As with many of John Malone's transactions, this one was extremely complicated, and the prospectus ran to several hundred dense pages. Gordy read the huge document at least three times. Hidden in the addendum to the prospectus was a table where TCI outlined its own estimate of the real value of each of the properties to be included in Liberty Media, and Gordy noted that the new shareholders would receive an amazing 35 percent liquidity discount from that level.

Gordy knew that John Malone could become one of the largest holders of the new public company, based on the information in the offering material, and his instinct told him that he and his associates should exercise all the rights they could, which would give Capital funds about a 13 percent ownership in the new firm, comparable to its TCI position.

Whether it was the sheer lack of understanding on the part of TCI's stockholders or a suspicion that Malone had saddled the company with too much debt, only about a third of the rights to purchase the new company's stock were going to be exercised. Capital ended up owning an astounding 43 percent of Liberty Media, far in excess of what the fund's internal ownership limits seemed to allow. It was also considerably more than Gordy had imagined possible, but he went back over all his projections for Liberty and felt confident that Capital Group should try to keep the entire block. His firm's lawyers reviewed the proposed purchase and determined that, because they were buying the less powerful shares, the transaction did not violate Capital's voting ownership limits. After an anxiety-filled few days, the transaction was complete.

Within two years, each share of Liberty initially acquired at $256 was worth $3,700; within five years, the price had appreciated twenty times! It was a career-defining trade for Gordy, who exhibited all the elements of sensible risk-taking. In particular, he was willing to take on the outsized weight in Liberty Media because he had spent so much time studying the offering documents, which detailed the asset values that John Malone, the company's CEO, one of the most astute media investors ever, was also buying in size.

Gordy was also very upfront about his biggest mistake, which was participating in and supporting the AOL Time Warner merger of 2000, which became the poster child for the Internet bubble. It still upsets Gordy that he had spent thirty years as a media analyst and investor who understood the dynamics of the entertainment, publishing, and cable industries, and then fell for a company about which he had little knowledge of the Internet side of its operations, which accounted for at least half the value. He was convinced by the AOL Time Warner management of the incredible opportunities of the combination, veering from his strengths and dismissing any cynicism. Unfortunately, none of those great synergies materialized, and the stock crashed and burned.

Gordy recovered and continued to have fantastic successes as a portfolio manager at Capital Group. Before he retired in 2012, his last significant act (along with a few of his associates) was buying 10 percent of Netflix at $60 a share after it had fallen from $300. He calculated that the company's streaming model would succeed globally but, like cable, at a steep near-term cost to the reported income statement. Netflix had a huge first-mover advantage, which it was exploiting very effectively, but that cost money in the near term. Gordon Crawford made an excellent and incredibly sensible trade: the stock has appreciated more than tenfold since that purchase.

The masters of my industry have an innate sense of risk-taking from which the rest of us can learn by observing. They rely on their understanding of the companies and sectors in which they invest and are instinctively skeptical of other people's forecasts until they do their own analysis. Peter Lynch, George Vanderheiden, and Gordon Crawford made significant bets over decades, decoding data that the market had yet to accept as meaningful. They recognized the enormous potential in investments ranging from motor inns, casinos, and banks to semiconductors, cable systems, and video content streaming services, while sizing and timing their risks carefully and fearlessly.

PART 4

Life

CHAPTER 13

Adversity

We face degrees of risk all day long. When we hit the snooze button, hang out with the kids at breakfast, or read another article in the paper, we know that there is a risk of getting caught in much worse traffic than if we had just gotten ourselves out of bed and on our way to work ten minutes earlier. The cost of being stuck in traffic is annoying but not detrimental, unless we have an important meeting at 8:00 a.m. and that extra shut-eye might jeopardize our attendance. My colleagues have often shared the thoughts they have during their morning commutes, revealing musings such as whether they have left the dog outside, if the back door may still be open, and whether it is worth passing a bus while commuting by bike.

Risk assessment starts early in our lives. A sixth grader who skips her math homework to watch TV faces public embarrassment if she is called on in class, and possibly her parents' anger if they find out she lied to them about completing all her assignments. I often wondered whether I needed to prepare for a business school case assigned for tomorrow if I had just been cold-called by the professor in class today. I was not a perfect student, that's for sure, but the possible shame of admitting to not reading the case was more than I wanted to risk, and this informed my study habits. This attitude was not shared by some of my peers, who played the odds and blew off studying for a class if they'd been called on the previous day.

My assessment was that the chance was small that I would be called on again, but the penalty for not reading the case and being exposed could be a failing grade. An extra hour or so of free time was not worth that risk.

BULLY BACK

We weigh costs and benefits throughout our lives. When Helen Foster,* now a senior partner at a top New York law firm, became pregnant before graduating from law school, she told the partner who had led the recruiting process right away. The firm was very understanding and placed her in the mergers and acquisitions group, led by one of the top attorneys in the field. She understood that after her maternity leave she might return to that group or be assigned to another. Helen would be working closely with several associates who had a few years of experience in that department.

Unfortunately, she soon began to hate her interactions with Randy Blunt,† one of the associates closest to the managing partner in the division. Even worse, Helen's office was directly across a small hallway from Randy's, so she could hear every word of his loud conversations.

Helen sensed that, for some reason, Randy did not like her or simply considered her a nuisance. All the firm's partners, with one exception, were male, as were three-quarters of the associates. She understood that Randy wasn't used to dealing with women at work as equals. Therefore,

---

* Helen Foster is a pseudonym.
† Randy Blunt is a pseudonym.

Helen tried every tactic, from asking for advice and soliciting his opinion, which most people take as flattering, to offering her thoughts in a group discussion while looking at him to elicit his support. Randy never even glanced her way.

For a couple of months, Helen tried to ignore Randy ignoring her. By late August, however, her pregnancy was showing and the problems really started. Randy began to insult Helen and call her names within earshot. He called her a cow, a fat pig, and much worse. When he was on the phone and Helen was in her office, she could hear Randy pepper his phone chats with comments such as "The cow just walked into her office."

Helen never told anyone at work. No one. She was afraid that if she did, she would risk gaining a reputation as a troublemaker, or worse, a liar. The early eighties was a time before sexual harassment became a term synonymous with offensive behavior, and before gender equality became a goal for both women and the corporations that hired them. Her superiors had no experience or training in handling a charged situation such as this. Helen did not blame them for not jumping to her defense. They probably never noticed and would have been too uncomfortable to address the issue if they had.

Randy predated Helen by years, he was very close and valuable to the managing partner in the mergers group, and he seemed to have plenty of support at the firm, even if it derived from his intimidating style of human relations. It might be worth noting that no one would ever accuse Helen of being overly sensitive. She can take ribbing and can dish it out. This was much different—mean spirited and vitriolic. One evening, after she had overheard Randy invoking her in a truly disgusting way, she went home and began to cry, relaying to her husband, Paul, what was going on at the office. Helen told him that she could not take any more abuse. She didn't know what to do, but needed to do something.

Paul gave her great advice. He said that Randy was a bully and Helen needed to bully him back. He told her to march into his office the next day and tell him that if he insulted her once more he would regret it. Helen laughed at that. What was he talking about? She did not know anyone whom she could ask to rough up Randy, nor did she think her husband did. Paul wore a suit to work every day and dealt with well-heeled customers.

Paul replied that follow-through was not the point. Helen had to walk into Randy's office, look him in the eye fearlessly, deliver the message, and then turn and walk right out. She wasn't sure she could do it. What if he laughed at her and the insults worsened? He could make her life even more miserable. The truth was that she was already miserable and so preoccupied at work that she was risking productivity along with her job. Helen could not let Randy irreparably damage her career. It was clear that no one was coming to her defense, so she had to act. The strategy struck her as both immature and thuggish, but she had no choice; she decided to follow Paul's advice.

The next day Helen had her chance. She and Randy were in a meeting together, reporting on the progress of a case in which they were both involved. When it was her turn to speak, Randy turned to the associate on his right, whispered something, and rolled his eyes. After the meeting, when Helen and Randy were both back in their offices, Helen told herself she could do it, took a deep breath, got up, and walked across the hall. She moved close to Randy's desk, looked him in the eye, and said, "Randy, if you ever, and I mean *ever*, insult me again, you will come to regret it. Don't test me." Then she turned and walked back to her desk, sweating.

It was very quiet across the hall. Helen waited five, then ten, minutes, but heard nothing. After that day, Randy never insulted Helen again. He occasionally spoke to her, although they never discussed her threat or what preceded it. Randy even asked how the baby was doing when she returned from maternity leave. A few years later, he left the company and moved to Los Angeles.

If a situation becomes untenable, and you have exhausted all obvious options, you sometimes have no choice but to act. Helen determined that she had no recourse but to act immediately, because Randy's attacks were only escalating in proportion to her weight. She was losing focus and confidence at work. One might argue that Helen should have spoken to a senior partner or tried again to reason with Randy, but there was no evidence that either would make a difference, and there was a risk that those actions would be either destructive or ineffective.

I am a strong believer that it is best to try to solve your own problems before moving on to the next level. Helen Foster did just that. The timing of her action was not bold or brash, but was carefully planned. An element of right timing is acting out of calculation rather than out of anger or impulse. Her plan did work, but if it had failed, she still had the option to approach her superiors. She considered whether Randy would complain to their boss or anyone else about her "threat," but felt that he was too much of a chauvinist to cry about being afraid that a seven-months-pregnant woman was going to hurt him.

FULL HOUSE

When my twins, Emma and Michael, were a little over two, and I was thirty, I became pregnant again. We were excited to have another baby and an ultrasound showed that this time I was only having one. In 1986, I was covering the media and entertainment stocks, managing the Leisure and Entertainment Fund, as well as the Broadcast and Media Fund. We had moved to the suburbs because the babies had been sleeping in the living room of our downtown apartment for two years, and it was getting a little ridiculous to be whispering all the time after 7:30 p.m. unless we were in our bedroom.

I worked full time, but we had a live-in nanny and three grandparents in the area who were very helpful. We were busy with two children and knew that with three we would most certainly be busier, but we felt ready to tackle the bedlam. I did not view this pregnancy as placing my career at great risk.

When I was five months pregnant, I had a routine blood test that showed irregular results, so my doctor asked that I come in for an ultrasound. As I lay on the cold table with that awful jelly-covered strobe circling my belly, I looked at the screen and experienced the biggest aha moment of my life.

"There's two in there," I screamed at the technician, who snapped her head from the screen to me and back.

"Wow! You're right," she replied. "Congratulations. You're having twins!"

Those were words that changed my life. "I have twins already," I said. "Just tell me there aren't three in there," I cried out in what could only be described as desperation.

Everything that happened in the next twenty-four hours remains a blur. I tore off the electrodes and called David to yell at him, as if he had made some terrible mistake. He came to get me and I think we went directly to see a psychiatrist friend of his who tried to calm me down. I could not see straight. Suddenly, I envisioned my life as career-less and uncontrollable rather than merely a more hectic version of the present.

My mother told me I needed to stop working for a while, whatever time frame that involved. Four children aged three and under! I did not want to think about the implications for my professional life, which was very important to my identity. But how could I leave our very own day-care center in the hands of…who? Having a couple of years of experience with nannies, I was well aware that finding solid child care for two infants or toddlers was not a cinch, regardless of salary. I decided not to talk to anyone else about the upcoming twins, particularly at work; I had some time to think this through.

I saw clearly the risk to my career if I stopped working. I also tried to imagine the risk to my family if I worked incredibly long hours and traveled incessantly. Neither option struck me as particularly positive.

A week later, I was on my way to Los Angeles to visit some film companies. The plane made a scheduled stop in Chicago, and I watched as a familiar-looking, well-dressed woman made her way toward me, seating herself in the first-class cabin two seats to my left. I knew that I had seen her face recently and was running through the alphabet to come up with her name, when she pulled a large manila envelope from her briefcase and emptied out about fifty letters. It was Ann Landers, the famous advice columnist. I knew that she lived in Chicago, and I also remembered that this was not her real name.

Incredible, I thought to myself; I can ask advice from a real expert. However, I did not want to address her by her pen name if I could retrieve her real name. I looked surreptitiously at those letters, concentrated, and amazingly came up with it—Eppie Lederer.

"Excuse me, are you Mrs. Lederer?" I asked, not knowing whether she was married but taking a chance.

"Yes," she replied kindly.

"Would you mind talking to me, please," I said, "because I have a problem."

Mrs. Lederer looked straight at me and, in a moment that I will never forget, she patted the seat between us and said, "Of course, dear, why don't you sit right here and we'll talk about it."

The following four hours were among the most important of my life. I explained that I had my heart set on a career, that I was very ambitious, loved my husband and family, but I had twins who were two and another set coming in a few months. I did not know what to do.

She said that my goal was to find contentment with my situation and to transmit that happiness to my family. If that meant using my entire salary to hire two nannies or however many people we needed so that no one, including David and me, were too tired to have a smile on our face when one of the children asked us to read a book, then we had to do that. If one of the children required more time and attention, I would have to adjust my schedule and, perhaps, my life. Most importantly, Ann Landers herself—one of the most highly considered oracles of personal problems—had given me hope that my career wasn't over. Mrs. Lederer also told me that I must not pay attention to the disapproval I would invariably face from people critical of my choice to work.

I helped her with her luggage coming off the plane, we exchanged business cards, and she urged me to stay in touch. Just to cover all the bases, I made an appointment with Sam Bodman, the president of Fidelity Investments, number two to our chairman, Ned Johnson. Without explaining that I was having twins, I asked if I might work part time for a while after my maternity leave. Sam looked at me compassionately and told me the job was only full time, and if I wanted it, I needed to fulfill this requirement, but in the same breath asserted he would make it worth my while. We have joked about that interchange since, because he sure held up his end of the bargain. I heard him loud and clear. I knew then that I had to right size my commitment to Fidelity without shortchanging my family. If it wasn't working a year later, I promised David, who was very supportive, I would rethink my strategy.

After Will and Andy were born, I took six months off without looking at the market, not that I did not think about it, but I was too busy and probably asleep whenever I had a free minute. Then, I told my boss at Fidelity that I would be returning and wanted to start learning my next industry group. By the time I was back, full time, after Labor Day 1986, I had hired two full-time nannies, an au pair, and a young local woman, Linda Williams, who worked for us for twenty-four years. The day before I restarted, I called Mrs. Lederer and told her what I was doing, receiving her well wishes in return. In that era, I truly believe I would not have succeeded in becoming a fund manager of a large fund if I had either taken a multi-year leave of absence or worked part time. There was no precedent or policy for mothers, since I was the only female in the research department who had any children, never mind four. That has changed dramatically over the years, but in 1986, I pushed my allowance for maternity leave as far as I could before coming back to work.

I tried my best to control my travel and to group company visits together rather than in separate trips. My hours were not as lengthy as those of most of my male colleagues. I was in the house to get the kids up and moving in the right direction for school and returned home at a reasonable hour. If my career suffered for it, the damage was not permanent, and I tried hard, as Eppie Lederer had advised, to maintain an air of relative contentment at home. Before anyone begins to think that I consider myself a model of great work–life balance, let me state right here that I am no one's model of well balanced but my own. I have been a hard-working investment professional who hopes desperately that I have been a good wife and mother.

Mrs. Lederer and I stayed in touch. Occasionally, I would meet her at the Helmsley Palace on Madison Avenue in New York for tea when we were both in town, or in Los Angeles, where she had a "beau." I even visited her beautiful apartment overlooking Lake Michigan, in Chicago. Once she asked me to review her portfolio, an impressive group of stocks she had accumulated for herself over the years.

She gave me advice that I believe changed my life. The stakes were high: my career and my identity. I was an ambitious young woman who had never expected four children by the time she was thirty, but life throws you curves, and this one was Sandy Koufax–worthy. There was nothing more serious to me at the time than applying some sensible consideration to this challenge.

The timing of our encounter was fortuitous. I could not have devised a more right-timed meeting than the one with Eppie Lederer, when I was in my third trimester with my third and fourth children. I desperately needed a strategy. She urged me to remain vigilant to reading the pulse at home. I knew I would apply myself to my job, but I needed to maintain a full awareness of my impact everywhere. Finally, she advised me to be skeptical of other people's opinions of my choices. I always tried to be careful not to judge the "How do you possibly do it?" comment as negative, but to smile and reply that I have a wonderful and supportive family. That was the truth.

Helen's encounter with Randy and mine with Eppie Lederer differed dramatically but they both highlight certain applications of risk-taking. Once we hit a critical junction, we need to act so that we don't lose focus. We need to avoid the risk of impulsivity and plan our responses thoughtfully. When approaching risk, act out of calculation, a component of right timing, and be open to advice from a trusted source.

.

CHAPTER 14

High-Wire Act

know many people who have intentionally taken on serious risks as investors, as company founders, as business executives, or in their personal lives. Sometimes they fail to grasp the worst-case outcome, eschewing the application of sensible risk-taking. There is no substitute for carefully considering the most negative scenario and how it might affect your life, and whether that pit in your stomach is a sign worth heeding.

ANOMALY

Gary Belthorpe* doesn't seem like a huge risk taker. He has a pleasant face, is of average height and weight, dresses with complete indifference, and wears shoes that are much too close to sneakers for his high-profile job. Despite having been a star on Wall Street for decades, he lacks any

---

*Gary Belthorpe is a pseudonym.

suggestion of swagger. Gary often pauses so long before responding that you wonder if he heard the question. When he finally begins to speak, he often looks down, cupping his head in one hand, as if the floor might offer some inspiration. Most people would label him a "nerd" who could be great with numbers, but not someone with a large appetite for taking bets and a track record that kept him in the high-stakes betting game for thirty years.

I met Gary shortly after I was assigned to manage the Select Biotechnology Fund at Fidelity in 1992. One of my colleagues told me that he was an amazing yet unusual resource, a Los Angeles–based biotech research analyst for a small brokerage firm. Nearly all the research support that Fidelity analysts and fund managers used in those days came from New York investment banks such as Goldman Sachs or Lehman Brothers, or even San Francisco–based companies, since the Bay Area was home to multitudes of players in this new industry.

Gary was an anomaly in ways other than geographical, although his early life was similar to many Wall Street success stories. Originally from a lower-middle-class Jewish family in New Jersey, he received a full scholarship to Columbia and then completed his doctorate in mathematics at Stanford in 1970. Among Gary's friends at Stanford were many future founders of biotechnology companies.

After a couple of years working in the math department at UCLA, Gary changed direction entirely. A gifted musician, as are many mathematicians, he accepted a job at an ad agency in Los Angeles, penning jingles for commercials. He transitioned to songwriting and collaborated on several hit pop tunes in the 1980s. Nearly thirty years after writing these songs, Gary still receives residuals each time they air on the radio.

After a decade in the entertainment business, Gary decided that he could risk switching careers again. He had made and saved a lot of money. At this point, he and his wife, a successful accountant, were raising their son and daughter in West Hollywood, and Gary was getting bored with jingles and excited about stock trading.

Gary moved toward embracing his proficiencies in math and science, this time with an eye to applying them by investing in the emerging biotechnology industry. He was fascinated by the intrinsic complexity of the human organism and how this relatively new discipline could engineer the molecules that might enhance, intercept, or redirect a human biological process in need of repair. Gary studied immunology, virology, molecular biology, and the manufacturing process through which yeast and Chinese hamster ovary cells manufacture drugs.

Where Gary excelled, in a manner unparalleled by all other industry analysts, was in working out the probability of a drug achieving the statistical significance in its human trials needed to warrant Food and Drug Administration approval. The agency wants to be at least 95 percent sure that any benefit for the drug-treated patients is unrelated to chance. In other words, that randomness plays no more than a 5 percent role in the outcome.

In the biopharmaceutical industry, achieving statistical significance is such a daunting task that the vast majority of new clinical entities entering the first, or Phase 1, human studies fail long before they get close to a Phase 3 conclusion. Drug companies like Merck and Lilly are loaded with PhDs hired to create a clinical design structure that will move the new molecular entities successfully through the regulatory system. Gary sought to apply his understanding of statistics, probabilities, and molecular biology to evaluating an industry in which risk-taking on new chemical compounds is the only pathway to product development.

When I met Gary, he was still working in Los Angeles as a research analyst for a small investment banking firm. To bolster our research for the Biotechnology Fund, Fidelity paid Gary's company in exchange for his research assistance. Since the future of most of these corporations rested on the back of their lead drug candidate, I was grateful for help in evaluating their prospects.

SHORTING THE SHOTS

Gary was the best in the business. He knew the science, but more importantly, he knew how to analyze the design and results of a clinical study. He also knew where to look for flaws and when to be most skeptical. If a study on an asthma drug shows twice the benefit for patients in New England that it does for patients in the rest of the country, Gary would note that there were twice as many pulmonologists in the Northeast, which could bias the outcome.

Gary taught me how to apply cynicism when faced with the uncertainty of a drug's effectiveness. Companies use MRI technology to detect the presence or absence of infection. If images of patients' lungs after treatment with a new antibiotic revealed a 70 percent decrease in infections, Gary would ask whether those patients who "looked" better on a screen also reported feeling better and were subsequently going to work or school more. The improvement in a surrogate marker might not be sufficient evidence of efficacy, in which case the company would have to conduct a different study with lower odds of success. I became skilled at dissecting drug trials and handicapping the impact on the related stock thanks to the hundreds of hours I spent tearing data apart with Gary.

To learn as much as we could, we often attended medical and science conferences together, staying until the conclusion of a breakout session to talk to the investigator about a drug's mode of action or the competition, all of which was public information but often difficult to decipher. When Gary thought a drug would work, based on the information we had gathered, he was almost always correct, and he was likewise correct when he concluded it would fail.

Gary used his research to augment his income, and became a hugely successful investor in his own right. His returns were incredible, particularly on the short side. Short sellers bet that a stock price will fall. If Gary's analysis indicated that the drug would not work, he might short the stock. If we worked on the research together and Fidelity did not own any of the stock, I was allowed to short the same stock. Gary's bets were always larger than mine, so much larger that I didn't know how he could sleep. During those years, my returns on these shorts were outstanding. One year, Gary's returns surpassed 4,000 percent. He always remained cynical of forecasts unless he could validate them himself, and he only invested when his own knowledge felt complete. He never placed a bet unless he was sure.

Gary's most successful short of the 1990s was Centocor, a Wall Street darling whose lead compound, Centoxin, was a treatment for sepsis. This often-fatal condition is characterized by the presence of harmful bacteria that cause the body's organs to shut down. Antibiotics were the standard of care but are not particularly effective. The biggest challenge in developing a single agent to treat sepsis was that it was not really a disease but a condition. Every patient who experienced sepsis was also suffering from another illness, such as cancer, or some shock to the system, such as burns or trauma.

Both Centocor and a rival, Xoma, were conducting clinical trials using an engineered monoclonal antibody to bind and inhibit the production of a type of protein called cytokines. These cytokines contributed to the inflammation process, which led to sepsis, and the prevailing notion was that inhibiting them would block the entire cascade and save patients' lives.

These two companies were embroiled in a vicious patent dispute over a similar antibody. Gary read through all the available animal and human trials, becoming convinced that any perceived benefit was a mere fluke. He uncovered animal studies in which the majority of dogs died and a public brief from Xoma's lawyers describing a baboon study in which none of the animals survived after being treated. The Wall Street community ignored this data, but Gary knew it was relevant. The pathophysiology of sepsis was too poorly understood at the time to dismiss clear evidence that the drug did not work.

In early 1992, despite a positive FDA Advisory Committee meeting on Centocor's drug, Centoxin, Gary bet against the stock. He sold short forty thousand shares at around $60 per share. After a series of setbacks, including an announcement by the FDA that there was insufficient data to support an approval and the halting of a European study, the stock plunged 90 percent, to $6.63. Gary made a profit of more than $2 million dollars. However, his sixteen-hour workdays, along with constant travel, ultimately led to Gary's marriage falling apart.

In 1995, Gary was recruited by a much more prestigious Wall Street firm, and he left Los Angeles for New York. By the late-1990s he had amassed a considerable fortune from both his multimillion-dollar salary and his personal stock trading. Although I had moved from managing biotech and health-care funds to a large diversified fund, we still spoke regularly.

Biotech, along with technology, Internet, and telecom shares became the proxies for market euphoria in 1999. During this period of wild optimism, when prices shot higher and higher, Gary stayed clear of betting against any stocks. After the market crashed in 2000, he was well positioned to jump back into the short end of the pool. This time, however, Gary failed to adhere to the risk-taking tenets he'd previously followed so closely.

CRATER TO ROCKET

Gary watched with interest the clinical progress of tadalafil, a drug for erectile dysfunction being developed by Icos, a biotechnology firm begun by George Rathmann, a cofounder of Amgen, and David Blech, an industry entrepreneur with an ambiguous reputation. Blech was a well-known biotech stock promoter who had been under investigation for stock manipulation in 1998, and was forced to shut his Blech & Co brokerage firm.[1] He was ultimately sentenced to four years in prison for securities fraud in 2013, but a decade earlier he was considered a discerning investor with notable start-ups such as Celgene and Neurogen.

However, his latest collaboration with industry giant Rathmann caused biotech investors to salivate.

Gary never believed that tadalafil would gain approval. Viagra was already available for the same indication, and lifestyle drugs were never at the top of the FDA's priority list. In addition, as anyone who has watched a Cialis ad knows (Cialis is the trade name for tadalafil), there are many disquieting side effects. Cialis has a considerably longer half-life in the blood than Viagra, possibly extending the "treatment benefit" for several hours, which is not necessarily desirable. Sudden hearing loss and blindness are also symptoms that we have heard recited at break-neck speed and which were made public following the Phase 3 studies. Despite the fact that the drug clearly worked, Gary was convinced that the FDA would deny approval.

He began shorting Icos in the late summer of 2003 at around $30 per share. It gyrated up and down, as often happens in the months preceding a potential approval date. Gary increased his short position to one of the largest he had ever held, 120,000 shares. Icos stock began to move higher in September. Gary doubled down. He was now in an incredibly high-risk position relative to his net worth.

When you buy stock you can only lose the value on the date of purchase. If you buy one hundred shares of a stock at $10, you can only lose $1,000.

Shorting is very different. When you bet that one hundred shares of a $10 stock will fall, you can theoretically lose an infinite amount of money because there is no limit to the future upside price of that stock. The short seller has borrowed stock, which he must return to the lender sometime in the future, hopefully at a much lower price. However, that eventual purchase price could be many multiples of where the stock was priced originally.

Gary's shorts had worked out so well in the past that he had never been caught in a "short squeeze," where the lenders begin asking for their stock back and the short seller must buy shares in the open market—generally at a much higher price than where they started, and in such volume that they push the price up ever further.

Icos moved into the high thirties and eclipsed $40 a share. Now Gary wasn't sleeping. He was getting squeezed and needed to put more cash into his margin account to appease the broker holding his position. In November 2003, the FDA did the inconceivable: it approved Cialis. The stock closed above $43, at which point Gary had to accept defeat and subsequently cover his entire position. He had personally lost almost $2 million on this single bet. At the same time, although perhaps not as a direct result, his second marriage, which quickly followed his first divorce, also disintegrated.

Over the course of our relationship, I have occasionally inquired about what went wrong. Why did he place such a large wager while simultaneously totally ignoring well-known aspects and fundamentals of sizing relative to his net worth? Upon reflection, he recognizes several aspects of this trade that differed dramatically from his other shorts. In the past, he'd applied his mathematical and scientific ability to analytically determine whether a clinical trial would show positive results during trials, consistently adhering to his rigorous methodology.

In this case, Icos had already proven that the drug worked. Gary had moved away from his core competency. He believed that the FDA would not approve a second lifestyle drug very similar to Viagra, but he misunderstood the agency's mission, one of which is to provide doctors and patients with multiple treatment options. Finally, Gary thought the side effects would derail the approval. He had never before based a short on the side effect profile of a drug, which proved to be a severe miscalculation.

Gary's past successes clouded his usually logical evaluation of risk. Not only did he stray from his strength in analyzing clinical data, but he placed a wrong-sized bet well outside his comfort zone. He was also distracted by his marital problems and should have recognized that he was not able to focus as clearly as such intellectual challenges required. While it seems unlikely that a math whiz would be so cavalier about the millions he could lose on a single bet, he simply suspended logic—a common affliction of gambling. In addition, every good investor I know has held out the belief that a losing position will turn around.

Despite this huge loss, Gary was not deterred. About the same time he made his Icos bet, Gary purchased a large position in Philip Morris at around $7 per share. The stock had been decimated from the tobacco industry's $100 billion settlement with attorneys general across the country. Gary conducted exhaustive research on the company's financial viability, its assets, and all its geographic markets. He rejected the consensus claim that Philip Morris (ticker MO) would fall victim to the settlement payments. While smoking in Western countries was in decline, emerging market consumption was on the rise. He tried to convince me to buy MO stock too, but I could not bring myself to buy cigarette stock. That might have been a mistake.

This trade, which looked frightening at the time, turned out to be the greatest windfall of his investing career. Philip Morris changed its name to Altria, and has subsequently risen to $50 per share. Two food companies, Kraft and Mondelez, spun out of Altria, as did Philip Morris International, adding over $160 of value for each of his original Philip Morris shares. Combined, Gary's $7-per-share investment is now worth $210 per share, a return of 2,900 percent over twelve years, not including the generous dividend payments.

Gary also married again, this time wedding a woman with a serene temperament who totally understands and appreciates Gary's obsessive nature. This marriage has an enduring quality that I hope will persist. When I asked Gary whether his choice to disregard his usual methodology arose from his affinity for risk-taking, he offered me an interesting perspective on the topic:

> I think some people probably take too many risks and some take too few risks. The extent to which you are gambling is not necessarily determined by the outcome. My two grandfathers took great risks coming to America with nothing in their pockets, leaving modest but stable lives in Poland. In some ways, that was a huge gamble into the unknown. Both of them invested in real estate, lost a lot of money in the Depression, but then made

it all back to lead very comfortable lives. On the other hand, my grandfather's brother opted to stay in their nice town in Poland where he owned a lovely house and had a very good business. He, his sisters, and their families all died in the Holocaust.

We need to apply a consistent framework to our risk-taking analysis and avoid complacency. Previous successes certainly do not ensure future returns, as every brokerage firm reminds us on every advertisement it broadcasts. When we stray from our risk-taking skill set, we increase the odds of losing money, reputation, and self-esteem. Gary fortunately returned to his roots of deep analysis and skepticism about consensus opinions that had made him successful in the first place.

CHAPTER 15

Running

In the course of our normal activities, we all face risks—but the scope of these risks does not usually justify changing our regimen, and we make programmed decisions regarding these risks almost unconsciously. I often begin my day facing risk when I head out of my house to run at 5:30 a.m., when it is still dark and cold. Many people tell me that I am crazy, running at such an early hour. Someone could jump out of the bushes in my suburban neighborhood and assault me.

To the friends and acquaintances who warn me, I am risking my life. I would downscale that to a scraped knee. In thirty-plus years of running I have never encountered anyone or anything objectionable, unless you count the stoned or drunk kids asleep on a bench after a Saturday night of partying. I have always had at least one springer spaniel as a running companion, and I trust that the dog would protect me. Fortunately, we have never had to test that theory.

I actually worry more that my dog, Jillie, who runs off the leash, will dart into traffic and be hurt or killed. We only cross one reasonably busy street on our way to the reservoir that we circle a few times, and she has always listened to my commands to stay and go. At this point, she is thirteen and a half years old, far advanced in springer longevity, and if something happened, we would all say at her memorial gathering that Jillie died doing what she loved best.

There is a risk that a police officer cruising by will issue me a citation, or whatever the violation is, for an unleashed dog. In all these years, I have only been stopped once and the officer merely advised me that I was not in compliance with the town's law. I thanked him for that information but never saw him again, although I see many police officers drive by who, fortunately, realize they have a more important mission than chastising a woman jogging with her dogs.

I risk smashing into or tripping over something hidden from sight in the dark. But I know my route cold and never vary from it even in the darkest of months. Of course, the fact that I run in quiet neighborhoods with few cars contributes to the darkness, but the only time I have hurt myself at all was when the town of Brookline built a sidewalk, seemingly overnight, where the street had transitioned smoothly into a pathway over a bridge. My foot smashed into the side of the step and I went flying, tearing up my shin. It hurt like hell, but I used some big leaves as Band-Aids and kept running. The scar was visible for a decade, but disappeared a few years ago.

The timing of my "risky" behavior is right, since I love being outside in the early morning, the quiet, and the chance to think—or even not to. It is also the best and easiest time of day for me to exercise. The cold almost never bothers me, although I am not one of those insane people who runs through snowstorms and wild weather conditions. I am a very experienced runner after all these years, and I get my knees checked every once in a while because of previous injuries. My early morning routine at home carries little risk.

However, when I traveled all over the world for Fidelity, I also ran in the predawn hours. I admit that this was riskier, because I was much less familiar with the terrain and sometimes got lost. The map I took from a concierge with scribbles that I could no longer read after it got sweaty inside my glove or sock usually became worthless, eliminating the "knowledge" component. I also sometimes had trouble finding English speakers that early in the morning. But even this did not fall under the heading of real danger but rather inconvenience, and, frequently, longer runs to find my way back. If the worst case was begging a security guard at the Imperial Palace in Tokyo to help me return to the Okura Hotel, the risk was worthwhile.

SURPRISING SECRET

I did not always run alone (other than with the dogs) but have had some intrepid, similarly inclined friends. My frequent running companion for years was Bob Gamere. For decades, before I ever met Bob, I knew who he was because he was the host of the popular *Candlepins for Cash* bowling show telecast in Boston when I was a teenager. Bob had a great mane of hair and rugged good looks, and he was also entertaining and knowledgeable, to the extent that bowling needed that level of interpretation. He had previously won the coveted job as a play-by-play announcer for the New York Yankees. The fact that he lost this and many other television positions speaks to his undeniable self-destructive streak. He was a career-wrecking alcoholic.

By the time we met in 1993, Bob had been hired and fired as a sports anchor at several local stations and was marginally employed. Nevertheless, he was always upbeat and quite the runner. He spent innumerable hours traversing greater Boston, stopping and chatting with tourists, students, and anyone else along his route who seemed interesting. He liked to jog early in the morning, did not mind the cold weather, and would meet me at a location that was convenient for me. We ran an hour or more two or three times per week for years, and trained and ran the Boston Marathon among numerous other races.

Bob was a wealth of knowledge and insight about sports, politics, and birds, and had an amazing memory for jokes. Since he once showed up at 5:30 a.m. reeking of alcohol, I gave him an ultimatum that if I could smell the alcohol, he was out of the picture and I would continue alone. He never arrived drunk again. We avoided talking about anything more personal than the occasional low-level drama with one of our kids. I never brought up the incident years before when he had been found, almost dead of several stab wounds, in the early morning hours near Fenway Park. I knew he was complicated and flawed, but he was at least as reliable as anyone else with whom I have ever participated in a sporting endeavor.

After a run on the morning of October 22, 2008, as we were about to run off in our separate ways, Bob hugged me. I thought it was odd, as he had never done that before. The stock market was in free fall so I thought he might have been trying to cheer me up. Two days later, I awoke to the clock radio's news at 5:16 a.m., and the first thing I heard was that former sports anchor Bob Gamere had been arrested for child pornography.

When I arrived at work, I called him, and he explained that he knew this was probably going to happen, which was why he embraced me. I asked him whether the charges were true, and he said that he had never touched a child inappropriately, or attempted to. This was not the kind of conversation with which I had any experience, so I ended it before we went on to what he did do.

RECKLESS OR CHARITABLE

A week after I learned of Bob's arrest, I received a call from a woman who identified herself as a federal court officer. She was calling about Robert Gamere's case. I asked how I could help and she said that the judge had offered Mr. Gamere a choice between jail confinement and house arrest, and Bob had asked whether he could go jogging. The judge scoffed at that, but Bob persisted and wanted to know whether he could run if he had a guardian or someone assigned to run with him. The judge asked who that might be, and Bob answered, "Karen Firestone." Bob's wife, Diane, insisted that I was unlikely to ever talk to him again, never mind run with him, but Bob said that the court should ask me anyway.

Rather than address the matter of how I felt about this suggestion, I asked the court officer everything that might be relevant. She told me that I would be required to vouch for Bob's whereabouts when he was out running, meaning that I had to be with him. He needed to be off the streets at 7:00 a.m. on weekdays and 7:30 a.m. on weekends. I could set the schedule, but needed to tell her or another court officer if the schedule changed, and I had to report any behavior not within this protocol.

I asked about the exact charges against Bob and she told me transmission of child pornography. Then I explained that I needed a few days to think about it and she replied, probably not for the first time, that he wasn't going anywhere. I promised to call her back soon. At that point, I needed to review what was at stake and ask the advice of a few people whose opinion I valued.

In terms of the risk to me physically, I dismissed that immediately. I had been running with Bob for fifteen years and he had never touched me other than the hug, by accident, or to pick me up off the ground on the day I fainted when I had a bad cold and had not slept the night before. People might think less of me for running with him, but how would they know unless I told them, and there was no reason to talk about it. There was a risk that Bob would try to escape while we were jogging, but I was sure he could not remove his tracking device and he just didn't seem like a flight risk to me. While he was in good shape, he was almost seventy and had slowed down significantly in the past few years.

What were the reasons to take on this assignment? Bob had erred horribly, but he had been my friend and had never done anything inappropriate to me. Much more important to me was the fact that running was the best part of Bob's daily routine; I did not want to be the person to deny him that activity, and I was in a position to do something very positive for him. I knew he hated treadmills, and if I said no, I did not think I could live with myself.

After a couple of days, I told the court officer that I would run with Bob Gamere on Tuesday, Thursday, and Sunday mornings, beginning the next day, but I would need to adjust the schedule to my vacation and weekend plans. She sounded somewhat surprised by my decision. Bob was obviously thrilled that I had agreed to take on that responsibility, but we rarely talked about the case. He described how he had been the subject of an FBI sting operation targeting visitors to a child pornography web forum who shared videos and photos. The implications of the charges disgusted me, and I would not listen to Bob complain about being set up. Occasionally, we reviewed his options of either a trial or a guilty plea, which carried a mandatory federal sentence of five years in prison.

His lawyers strongly recommended the latter, because jurors—particularly female jurors—rarely sympathize with child pornography defendants. The maximum sentence was twelve years, and Bob's attorneys worried that this outcome was possible if a jury found him guilty. We never spoke about how he felt about his situation, whether he felt remorse, or the effect on his family.

I felt truly sorry for his wife and three sons, all of whom had excellent jobs, and two of whom were married with children. Mostly, we stuck to our regular topics—whatever sports season was in progress, news stories, and local and national politics. During 2009, Bob gave me plenty of grief about being a part of the evil "Wall Street" empire that had nearly destroyed the world. It was ironic that he turned the tables so that I was somehow the guilty one.

We jogged through the winter, spring, and fall of 2009, still with no imminent sentencing date, but then Bob received notice of his court date in January 2010. He asked me to write a letter in his favor, not for leniency in the sentence, since that was fixed, but to request a prison relatively close to Boston. I went to the sentencing, which was the only time I have ever set foot in a federal courtroom, and I am not anxious to go back. There were cameramen outside snapping photos because Bob Gamere was still a recognized local celebrity. The uniformed officers led Bob away to begin his sentence in a prison several hundred miles away in rural Pennsylvania. So much for my influence.

When we communicated through the prison's e-mail system, I carefully reread my correspondence, knowing that someone else would read it before Bob. Once in a while, he called me about some major breaking story that he knew I would find interesting. I learned nothing about his life in prison other than the fact that he taught English to other inmates and that there was a makeshift track outdoors on which he ran every day, weather permitting.

When he and Diane moved out of Brookline upon his release, I fully understood. They now live even farther outside the city, with a huge state park and incredible running trails only a few hundred yards away.

I told very few people that I was a court-assigned "guardian runner" for a man ultimately sentenced to five years in prison for an awful crime. I suspect that most people who know me would not be shocked, and would agree that I was out jogging anyway, with or without Bob Gamere. If I had broadcast my activity, perhaps it would have hurt my reputation. Instead, it made me feel better about myself. I know it made Bob feel better. I probably face more risk today, running by myself again in the dark, than I did when I was running with Bob.

We sometimes face pressure to consider risk in some predetermined way, which would have led me to say no about running with Bob. However, that would have ignored an honest evaluation of my risks and the positive impact I would have on Bob's life. In addition, taking a risk you have calculated as small relative to the consensus, whether it is personal, professional, or an investment, can turn out to be very gratifying.

EPILOGUE

Our firm has weathered a financial crisis, hacking, and the daily investment uncertainties integral to the investment industry, but we have survived, grown, and passed the decade milestone. Despite our emergence from one of the most severe periods of economic turmoil in a generation, we at Aureus now face another set of decisions that will have implications across our business for years to come.

Much of our success is a result of our social structure, which has informed our culture from the very beginning. We will soon experience a dramatic shift as my cofounder and partner, David, becomes chairman emeritus and enters semiretirement. He has served as chairman since our inception, and represents, along with me, the origin of our enterprise. It was always clear that he would retire before me because of our age difference, but that seemed ages away. Until recently, I was both the CEO and president—taking on another "C" feels both greedy and selfish. Keeping them all might be a mistake and a risk to our firm.

Perhaps because we have been a female–male leadership team, David and I have aimed to build a friendly workplace environment in which collaboration is paramount and squabbles extremely rare. We respect and like each other, even when we have disagreements, but work incredibly hard to maintain strong investment results, since that is the reason we exist. This company's culture has produced a high level of employee retention throughout our history.

I know each of the people in the running to replace David well, and will consider how each has handled critical tasks and how he or she is likely to respond to more pressure and interaction with colleagues. I am reviewing the complete process through which we developed and implemented different investment and client-specific programs to compare the different styles of our partners. I know that my closest advisors and I share a sensibility about our company's direction, but also that they have independent voices. David and I had a wonderful collaborative relationship in which we often debated and challenged the validity of each other's thinking, but we eventually found common ground on every major decision.

I need to be cynical about how well I truly understand the relationships among people in the office, and how a change of one or two titles will affect our internal dynamics. This includes me. Sometimes I argue with one of my partners, with whom I work very closely on stocks, about one stock or another in our portfolio. We always resolve the argument, but will this also happen with management issues? I would loathe adding more layers of administration that can reduce transparency and direct discussions between the individuals working on a project. Nearly all transitions—whether of stocks or executives—are less seamless than anticipated, and I question how easily we will be able to enact our changes. I will need to pay attention to many details about lines of responsibility and communications, and push my own limits of patience.

Over the course of my career and personal life, I have dealt with many high-pressure situations, as we all do. Risk is present in most major decisions. Developing the skill to both assess and tackle such uncertainty has been one of the greatest challenges in my life. I am enormously grateful for all the rich experiences that have shaped the way I see risk. The evolution of my approach toward sensible risk-taking is a product of the trials that come from the demands of life as an investor, parent, entrepreneur, and business leader. The legacies of such challenges are the tenets that have guided me in many decisions throughout my life.

ACKNOWLEDGMENTS

I am extremely grateful to the people who encouraged me to undertake this book-writing journey and urged me forward along the way. At Aureus Asset Management, my partner, Thad Davis, was my ardent supporter, always willing to discuss ideas, read portions of *Even the Odds*, and offer solid advice. All my other colleagues, with special thanks to Brennan Jones, Stacey Atkinson, and Stefan Karlsson, were uniformly positive and helpful with research, proofreading, and being generally good sports about my project over the past year.

Jonathan Hansen provided insightful feedback, sometimes painful, on every chapter I wrote. Without his clarity, organization, and optimism this book would not have been possible. I am deeply indebted to Giles Anderson, my agent, for his belief in me and my writing. I am eternally grateful to Erika Heilman, Jill Friedlander, Alicia Simons, and everyone at Bibliomotion for their enthusiasm and direction. My friend Shirley Mills courageously offered to read this book and heroically and carefully critiqued the entire manuscript. Peter Economy has been an ally and guide throughout this process. Thanks to all the people to whom I spoke and whose stories represent the framework for this book. I am grateful to all the songwriters, from Bach to Amy Winehouse and Keith Urban, whose music I played in the background as I worked; and to my trusty laptop, which miraculously, given my computer skills, never lost any of my words.

I especially thank my husband and life companion, David, who offered me valuable perceptions as this book progressed. Also, I am appreciative of my four children and my grandchildren for their love and inspiration. Finally, I want to thank my mother, Anita, who would have been very proud of this accomplishment.

NOTES

Introduction

1. *Encyclopedia Britannica* online, "Charles E. Merrill," accessed November 2, 2014, http://www.britannica.com/biography/charles-e-merrill.

Chapter 1

1. Ryan Dezember and Tess Styne, "Halliburton to Pay Nigeria $35 Million to Settle Bribery Case," *Wall Street Journal*, December 22, 2010.

Chapter 2

1. "Washington State Investment Board Selects Fidelity to Manage International Mandate," October 27, 2004, http://institutional.fidelity.com/about_us/news/washington.html.

Chapter 4

1. Colleen M. Faddick, "Health Care Fraud and Abuse: New Weapons, New Penalties, and New Fears for Providers Created by the Health Insurance Portability and Accountability Act of 1996 ("HIPAA")," *6 Annals of Health Law 77* (1997), http://lawecommons.luc.edu/annals/vol6/iss1/5.
2. "U.S. Department of Justice Health Care Fraud Report, Fiscal Years 1995 and 1996," October 27, 1997, http://www.justice.gov/opa/us-department-justice-health-care-fraud-report.

3. "Peak Prosperity," accessed April 15, 2015, http://www.peakprosperity.com/about.

4. Charles Hugh Smith, "The Fatal Flaw of Centrally Issued Money," April 9, 2015, http://www.peakprosperity.com/blog/92313/fatal-flaw-centrally-issued-money.

Chapter 6

1. Nassim Taleb, *Black Swan* (New York: Random House, 2010), xxii.

Chapter 7

1. Timothy Geithner, "Geithner's Speech to the Economic Club of Washington," Real Clear Politics, April 22, 2009.

2. Aureus company reports, generated by Advent Software.

3. Aureus company reports, generated by Advent Software.

Chapter 9

1. Michael Wallace, et al., "Warburg Dillon Read Report, Yahoo," January 18, 2000.

2. Youssef Squali, "Cantor Fitzgerald, Yahoo," May 20, 2015.

3. Bob Hiller and Daniel Lynch, "Credit Suisse Report on Yahoo," August 30, 2000.

4. Scott Ard, "Taking Stock of 1999: From e-Commerce to Linux to Wireless, 1999 Was a Banner Year. What's Ahead for 2000?," January 2, 2002, http://www.cnet.com/news/taking-stock-of-1999/.

5. Ard, "Taking Stock of 1999."

6. Timothy Dolan, "Deutsche Bank Report on Broadvision," September 21, 1999.

7. United States Census Bureau, "U.S Retail Trade Sales—Total and e-Commerce (1998–2013)," http://www.census.gov/retail/index.html.

8. United States Department of Commerce, "E-Stats," March 7, 2001, http://www.census.gov//econ/estats/1999/1999estatstext.pdf.

9. "Ecommerce Sales Topped $1 Trillion for First Time in 2012," *Emarketer*, February 5, 2013, http://www.emarketer.com/Article/Ecommerce-Sales-Topped-1-Trillion-First-Time-2012/1009649.

10. Allison Enright, "U.S. Annual e-Retail Sales Surpass $300 Billion for the First Time," February 17, 2015, https://www.internetretailer.com/2015/02/17/us-annual-e-retail-sales-surpass-300-billion-first-time.

11. U.S Department of Commerce, "U.S. Census Bureau News," November 17, 2015, https://www.census.gov/retail/mrts/www/data/pdf/ec_current.pdf.

Chapter 10

1. Aureus analysis and research.
2. Charles Arthur, "Ten Things to Know About Blackberry—And How Much Trouble It Is (or Isn't) In," *The Guardian*, September 29, 2014, http://www.theguardian.com/technology/2014/sep/29/ten-things-to-know-blackberry-john-chen.
3. Mark Rogowsky, "Without Much Fanfare, Apple Has Sold Its 500 Millionth iPhone," *Forbes*, March 25, 2014, http://www.forbes.com/sites/markrogowsky/2014/03/25/without-much-fanfare-apple-has-sold-its-500-millionth-iphone/.
4. "Nasdaq Net 1 UEPS Technologies, Inc. Stock Report," November 2, 2015, http://www.nasdaq.com/symbol/ueps/stock-report.
5. Aureus company reports, generated by Advent Software.

Chapter 11

1. Jason Napier, Allied Irish Banks Plc, "Allied Irish Bank FY2007 Earnings Review," Deutsche Bank, March 29, 2008.
2. Lauren Dugan, "Only Half of Twitter's Active Users Actually Tweet," *Social Times*, November 11, 2013, http://www.adweek.com/socialtimes/twitter-monthly-active-users/493019.
3. Doug Anmuth, et al., "J. P. Morgan Report," December 2, 2013.

Chapter 12

1. Aureus company reports, generated by Advent Software.

Chapter 14

1. Bob Van Voris, "David Blech Gets Four Years for Manipulating Stock Prices," Bloomberg Business, May 2, 2013, http://www.bloomberg.com/news/articles/2013-05-02/david-blech-gets-four-years-for-manipulating-stock-prices.

ABOUT THE AUTHOR

Karen Firestone is chairman, CEO, and cofounder of Aureus Asset Management. Previously, she spent twenty-two years at Fidelity Investments as a diversified fund manager and research analyst. She is a regular contributor to the Harvard Business Review blog and the Huffington Post. Ms. Firestone received a BA from Harvard College and an MBA from Harvard Business School. She and her husband live in Brookline, Massachusetts. They have four grown children and two grandchildren.

www.karenfirestone.com